In Defence of the Realm

PROTEUS BOOKS is an imprint of
The Proteus Publishing Group

United Kingdom
PROTEUS (PUBLISHING) LIMITED
Bremar House,
Sale Place,
London, W2 1PT

United States
PROTEUS PUBLISHING COMPANY
distributed by:
LIPPINCOTT & CROWELL PUBLISHERS, INC.
521 Fifth Avenue,
New York, NY 10017

ISBN 0 906071 31 3

First published in UK July 1980
© 1980 Proteus Publishing Group and Roger Reynolds
All rights reserved.

Typeset by Computacomp (UK) Ltd,
Fort William, Scotland
and printed and bound in Rome, Italy by
I.P.E. - International Publishing Enterprises s.r.l.

In Defence of the Realm

The British Royal Family as War Leaders

Roger Reynolds

PROTEUS

LONDON AND NEW YORK

IN DEFENCE OF THE REALM
A pictorial study of the changing role of British
royalty as war leaders. Over 200 photographs,
including 32 pages of colour. With a 35,000 word
commentary by historian *Roger Reynolds*.

Contents

The Welcoming Shore

Long before mankind entered the world stage, Britain was geographically a part of Europe's mainland, and Snowdonia and the Pennines formed the north-western crest of a massive valley which swept south-eastwards towards the mountainous regions of north and east France. Then angry seas split the valley asunder, and the British Isles, surrounded by water, faced the continent across the Channel and North Sea, her low-lying east and south coasts invitingly open to the nomadic tribes which began, much later, to roam the shores of the continental land-mass. These tribes crossed the waters to trade, to plunder and destroy, and to settle.

Early British (Iberian) man barely survived under that most simple political structure, the small tribal unit. He lived in constant fear of wild animals, like the bear and wolf, and of his warring neighbours; he dwelt in clearings in the huge forest that was Britain, and on the Chalk Downs of the south and east. Yet he was capable of magnificent engineering feats like Stonehenge and the huge earth-works at Maiden Castle. How this primitive being achieved such stupendous works remains beyond our comprehension.

In about the seventh century B.C. the blond, fierce Celts from north-west Germany and the Netherlands began to invade Britain across the Channel and the North Sea. They came in large numbers, driving the Iberians ever northward and westward before them. How many indigenous Iberians the Celts assimilated by slavery and subjugation, and how many they expelled and destroyed is unclear, but, as they settled, they followed the Iberian political structure, breaking into small tribal groups and, in turn, falling victim themselves to ensuing waves of Celtic invaders. This bizarre pattern repeated itself continually until about the third century B.C., when the invasions seem to have ceased, probably because the incumbent Celts had begun to realise the importance of the larger political unit as the key to defending themselves and their new homeland.

Julius Caesar landing in Britain (55 BC).

When Julius Caesar landed in 55 B.C., amalgamated tribes of Celts were living in land areas larger than most of the modern English counties, and were capable of forming confederacies with neighbouring tribes in times of crisis and trouble. The more successful tribes, possessing the richest agricultural lands to the south and east, offered the sternest resistance to Caesar, and the spearhead of this resistance was the Belgic tribe of Cattuvellauni under their strong king, Cassivellaunus.

Far Left
*Julius Caesar's troops
attacking Verulamium
(St Albans) (54 BC).*

Left
*Map of pre-Roman Britain,
showing distribution of the
tribes in the first century BC.*

Below Left
*Victorious Roman troops with
Celtic captives (55–54 BC).*

Right
*Maiden Castle, the prehistoric
earthworks showing the
Quadruple banks.*

*Stonehenge, the prehistoric
mystery.*

The Rise and Fall of Roman Britain

Coin showing the head of Magnus Maximus, last Roman leader in Britain (c. 383 AD).

Coin showing the head of the Emperor Hadrian (c. 122 AD).

Map of Roman Britain, showing Roman settlements and coastal forts.

Julius Caesar did not seek to conquer Britain for the Roman Empire in 55 and 54 B.C. The Belgic tribes of Gaul were receiving aid from their British kin in their fight against Rome, at a time when Caesar sought popularity at home. He saw an opportunity to both punish the British and obtain the treasure and slaves he needed to gain prestige in Rome.

The resistance by Cassivellaunus to the Roman legions was more than nominal, for the Cattuvellauni had, under his leadership, gained control of the Belgic tribes of southern Britain. He had to sue for peace in 54 B.C., however, because of betrayal by the non-Belgic tribes of the south, particularly the Trinobantes, who, jealous of his power, had sought an earlier truce with the Romans. The departure of Caesar saw a vengeful Cassivellaunus, determined to strengthen Britain against future Roman attacks, conquering the Trinobantes and setting up his Belgic capital at Camullodunum (Colchester).

The royal family of the Cattuvellauni, descendants of Cassivellaunus, built upon his achievements during the hundred years leading to the Roman invasion. In the year 5 A.D. the last and greatest king of the dynasty, Cunobelinus (romanticized by Shakespeare in *Cymbeline*) ascended the throne. He greatly increased the territorial possessions of the tribe by the constant conquest of lesser tribes and, on his silver coins, called himself 'Rex Brittanum' (king of Britain). During his life he remained the focal point of British resistance and the Romans did not invade, knowing that with his death his factious sons would divide the loyalties of the kingdom and make the conquest easier.

The death of Cunobelinus in 43 A.D. was the signal for invasion by the Emperor *Claudius* and his general Aulus Plautius. The resistance by Togodomnus and Caratacus, the royal sons of the dead British king, was short-lived, for, once again, the non-Belgic tribes, sensing the weaknesses, deserted the Cattevellauni on the eve of battle and negotiated a separate peace. The Romans, having defeated Caratacus at a battle for possession of the Thames' estuary, marched on Colchester. The power of the Belgic tribe was destroyed forever.

Caratacus brought before the
Emperor Claudius in chains
(c. 43 AD).

Cassivellaunus subjects
himself to Julius Caesar
(54 BC).

More serious resistance to the Roman conquerors came 17 years later when the Roman legions were destroying the Druid power in the west. Their erstwhile allies, the Iceni and Trinobantes, rose under the Iceni queen Boudicca and sacked the Romano-British townships of Colchester, London and St. Albans, massacring thousands. The revolt occurred because the Romans would not allow Boudicca to ascend the throne vacated by the death of her husband King Prastagus, wanting the tribe to subject itself totally to Roman rule. Boudicca coveted the crown for herself and her daughters, and the Romans seriously underestimated the loyalty of the Iceni to their royal family and to their determined queen. The Roman legions, hastening back from the west, destroyed the Iceni and Trinobantes in battle, and Boudicca took poison, but the Romans came close to losing control of Britain during this ferocious and serious revolt.

What distinguished Boudicca's rebellion and has captured the imagination of the British people ever since, is a combination of her femininity, her strong leadership in refusing to allow the Roman machine to crush her tribe without a fierce struggle, the total justice of her cause and the magnitude of the revolt which nearly overthrew the proud and mighty Roman conquerors. It is also sadly remembered for the cruel vengeance visited by the normally benevolent Romans upon the Iceni themselves, which destroyed the tribe, and upon their lands, now known as Norfolk, which were laid waste for generations to come.

For the next 350 years the defence of Britain remained in the hands of the Roman legions. The Romano-British, living peacefully in their villas and towns never had to take up arms. After the visit of the Emperor Hadrian in 122 A.D., the construction of the famous Hadrian's Wall began; it was built to keep out the raiding Iberians and Celts, who, refusing to submit to Roman rule, had fled north. Additional defensive measures were taken in the second century when the Saxons first began to raid the British shores. The Romans erected a series of coastal forts and built a fleet to patrol the Channel.

The Romans kept the invading Saxons at bay for almost 200 years after those first sightings, by use of the forts and the British fleet. But, by the end of the fourth century, the end of Roman rule was in sight. In 383 A.D. Magnus Maximus, a Roman officer stationed in Britain, declared himself Emperor of Rome, and, with the British legions, attacked the mainland of Europe. He conquered half of Europe before he was defeated in 387, but the legions never returned to the defence of Britain, and the Romanized British, never trained in the acts of warfare, were left to the mercy of the Saxon hoards, whilst the Roman Empire itself was disintegrating.

Left
Roman legions leaving the shores of Britain for ever (c. 383 AD).

Below
Building Hadrian's Great Wall, stretching from Solway to Tyne (122 AD).

Boudicca attacking Camullodunum (Colchester) (60 AD).

The Dark Ages and the 'Once and Future King'

We have little knowledge of our history during the so-called 'Dark Ages'. We do know, however, that the Angle and Saxon hoards attacked, devastated and comprehensively conquered the east of Britain. The evidence also suggests that they swept far into the west in those early years, destroying but not settling. After the initial Anglo-Saxon thrust, stories from the seventh and eighth centuries tell of a series of important British victories during the early years of the sixth century, culminating in a great and decisive victory for the British in 518 at an unidentifiable site, then called 'Mount Bladon'.

Story and legend also come down of a great king, named Arthur, who led the British forces to this series of triumphs. It seems likely that he did exist and that he was a Romano-British cavalry leader, which would explain how he could have been credited with victories the length and breadth of Britain, following quickly one upon the other. It is unlikely that the claim of the twelfth-century writer, Geoffrey of Monmouth is correct, and that Arthur was the son of Urther Pendragon, King of All The Britons.

The importance of the victory at Mount Bladon seems to be that it forced the Anglo-Saxons back to the south and east of Britain for one hundred years, there to consolidate their conquests and become civilized and politically organized, and left the north and west to the British. It gave both sides a period of peace and harmony in which to learn to co-exist.

Legend has it that Arthur is not dead but sleeps until he is called again to the defence of the realm, and that, on the stone which marks his resting place are inscribed the words, in Latin: 'Here lies Arthur, the once and future king'.

Imaginary statue of King Arthur in armour, (in Innsbruck).

King Arthur returning to Camelot (from a 16th century Flemish manuscript).

The Coronation of King Arthur (c. 500 AD?).

Arthur with his knights of the round table (from a fourteenth century French manuscript).

*Saxons raiding the East Coast
of Britain (c. 450 AD).*

The Struggle for Unity

During the seventh, eighth and early ninth centuries, the Anglo-Saxon kingdoms of England struggled for dominance over each other, the more far-sighted kings realising that they could not conquer the British until they were united. As early as 617 Edwin, King of Northumbria, could claim to be the 'Bretwalda' or 'over-king' of England, and his kingdom stretched as far north as Edwin's Burg (or Edinburgh, as it came to be known). His over-lordship did not last long, however, and soon his most powerful vassal kingdom, Mercia, was in revolt under its king Penda. Penda defeated and killed Edwin at the Battle of Heathfield in 633, heralding a twenty-five year struggle between the two kingdoms which climaxed in the death of the Northumbrian king, Oswy, in 659 and the permanent eclipse of Northumbrian power. Mercia emerged triumphant and, under the rule of the House of Penda, strengthened its position as the most powerful English kingdom over the next 150 years.

The royal family of Mercia produced a series of able kings, the most famous, and the last, being the towering figure of Offa II (757–796). He claimed direct descent from Offa I, who had reigned over the Angles in their former homeland of Schleswig four hundred years before and was also a direct descendant of Penda. Offa increased the power and prestige of his kingdom to the point where, reluctantly, the independent kingdom of Wessex acknowledged him as Bretwalda. The Pope addressed him, without qualification, as King of the English, and he was on close terms with his great contemporary, Charlemagne. He took the fight to the newly named 'Welsh' (which was the Anglo-Saxon word for 'alien') and ordered the greater earthwork, later known as Offa's Dyke to be constructed along his Welsh frontier. He crushed, unmercifully, all Anglo-Saxon opposition and, finally, in 793, killed the King of East Anglia and annexed his kingdom. Sadly for Mercia, Offa's heir was his sickly son, Ecgfrith, who survived his father by four months. The Mercian crown then went to a remote kinsman, Coenwulf, who could impose his authority on neither the vassal kingdoms nor his

Danish raiders bound for England (c. 800 AD).

Gold penny showing head of King Offa of Mercia (c. 790 AD).

own subjects. The fall of the House of Penda, and the fall of the kingdom of Mercia thus coincided.

Chronologically parallel with the dominance of the kingdom of Mercia, Wessex quietly consolidated its royal house and widened its frontiers. King Ine (688–726) was typical of the strong kings who spent the greater part of their reigns fighting against the British in the west. He set up his kinsman, Nunna as under-king in Sussex, and in about 705 ousted the British king Geraint from Taunton.

Whilst the struggles for over-kingship continued, England had been converted to Christianity by two opposing forces of the religion, the Celtic Christians from the north-west and the Latin Christians from the south-east. The victory of the Latins in the fight for supremacy over the English Church was important for they believed in centralised control and demonstrated to English kings how organised and efficient was the unified Church administered from Canterbury.

After Ine of Wessex, an unbroken series of able kings in that kingdom meant that Egbert could defeat the Mercians at Ellandune in the year 825, and establish Wessex as the most powerful kingdom. It was already too late, however, to defend the rest of England from the Danish invaders who had first been seen during the latter years of the reign of Offa II.

The Danish fleet sailing up the English Channel (c. 800 AD).

Alfred the Great, Guthrum and the Danes

In the seventy years following the death of Offa, the Danes triumphantly conquered the English kingdoms, successively taking East Anglia, Essex and Kent, then swamping decadent Northumbria and finally defeating declining Mercia, until, by 870, only Wessex stood between Guthrum, leader of the Danes, and total domination of England.

There then arose in Wessex the only king in English history to earn the title 'Great'. Alfred was chosen King of Wessex by the Witan in 871 at the age of twenty-two on the death of his brother, and in preference to his nephews who were still minors. He had shown qualities of leadership from an early age, and had proven himself in battle a popular and courageous war-leader.

The Anglo-Saxon Witan, or meeting of 'wise men', was an unrepresentative body chosen haphazardly from among the royal household and from influential landowners and churchmen; one of its major functions was to convene after the death of an Anglo-Saxon king in order to select his successor. The new king was chosen from within the ruling family and, often, out of respect for the dead father, the eldest son was chosen. This was by no means certain, however, and, if the son was a minor, the dead king's brother or cousin might ve chosen in his stead. In most elections the choice was clear, but when dispute arose, the choice of the Witan tended toward the most powerful, charismatic and wealthy contender, for without these qualities a man could not long remain king.

In 878 Alfred's fight against the Danes had reached its nadir. The Danes were raiding at will, and the King, with his kinsmen and a few retainers, was holding out in the fenlands of the west. He is there said to have had a vision which inspired him to summon his thegns to the royal banner for one final effort. Because of the quality of his leadership, they came from all over Wessex to his rallying call, and he won the decisive battle of Ethandine in brilliant manner. Following this victory, Guthrum signed the Treaty of Wedmore, leaving Wessex as an enlarged and independent Saxon kingdom, incorporating London and Kent. The Danes withdrew into their 'Danelaw' (formerly Northumbria, Mercia and

Alfred the Great attacking the Danes (c. 871–878 AD).

Essex) and Guthrum was converted to Christianity.

In the remaining years of his reign, Alfred continued to repel the Danes still invading from the continent, and he built the first English navy, which proved effective as less invaders reached the Wessex shores. He was a scholar and able administrator as well as a brilliant general, and he left the English a good administrative system for the first time in their history. Treason to the king was made the most heinous of crimes as respect for the Crown, personified in Alfred, grew in Dane and Anglo-Saxon alike. By the time he died peacefully in the year 900, the Danes had lost the political unity they had found under Guthrum's leadership, and had reverted to their former tribal states, whilst the Royal Family of Wessex was assured of the Crown for generations to come.

Statue of King Alfred at Wantage.

Portrait of King Alfred the Great (871–900 AD).

The Royal House of Wessex

King Edward of Wessex, son of Alfred, defeating the Danes at Watchet (921 AD).

The reconquering of the Danelaw was begun under Alfred's son Edward, (900–924), and his daughter, the Lady Ethelfleda of Mercia, and, because of the disunity of the Danes, easily completed by Alfred's grandson and Edward's heir, Athelstan (924–939). Athelstan could truly be described as the first King of All England, though the dominance of the Wessex family is best illustrated by that impressive historical day in 973 when eight vassal kings paid homage to King Edgar (959–975) by rowing him down the River Dee.

The centralisation of power in the hands of the royal family meant, paradoxically, that power had to devolve to other privileged Danish and Saxon families throughout the land who, in turn, were answerable to the central authority of the Crown. The King retained his power over the whole country for purposes of national defence, but for little else. Justice became the instrument of these 'earls' who now became almost autonomous in their 'shares' or 'shires'. In these times when the royal family was revered and respected, and the system suited both king and earl, it worked well, but the seeds of feudal England had been sown, and with the seed came the chaff which would cause so much bitter struggle for power between the medieval king and his barons.

The Royal House of Wessex began its decline when the weak, ineffectual Ethelred the Redeless more popularly known as 'the Unready', reigned for a disastrously long thirty-eight years (978–1016). Ironically it was the very popularity of his family that sustained this foolish and cowardly man on the throne for so long. Ethelred followed a policy of appeasing the invading Danes and bribing them away from the shores of England with Danegeld, a tax he extracted by force from his people. The amounts levied were so large that they can be regarded as causing the most significant social development of the age as impoverished freeholders were forced into the thralls of serfdom.

The nation became restless enough in 1013 for Sweyn, King of Denmark, to succeed in usurping the throne, but he died on the third of February 1014, and the Witan recalled and re-instated Ethelred. He finally died, generally unmourned, on the twenty-third of April, 1016.

Ethelred (the 'Redeless') levying Danegelt to bribe the Danes (991 AD).

Engraved for Russel's History of England.

Wale delin.

Walker sculp.

KING EDGAR *rowed down the* River Dee *by Eight Tributary* KINGS *attended by his principal Nobility.*

King Edgar of England being rowed down the Dee by eight vassal kings (973 AD).

29

A Dream of Nordic Empire

Portrait of King Canute (1016–1036).

The belated death of Ethelred heralded a short civil war waged between Edmund Ironside, son of Ethelred, and Canute, son of Sweyn. Canute triumphed and, with Edmund's death in November, 1016, was elected King by a Witan which bowed to the reality of his armed strength. At the age of twenty he had taken the first step toward realising his great ambition to forge a mighty Empire across the North Sea; four years later he took a further large stride when he wrested the Danish throne from his brother's weaker grasp.

In England, Canute continued to impose Danegeld, although at a lower rate, but he used it to augment the country's defences, not to bribe rapacious raiders. He substantially increased the size of the standing army and greatly strengthened the fleet.

Although he had acquired the throne of England by force and as a heathen, his policy of uniting the different races, and his wisdom during his twenty year reign, made him greatly loved and respected by all his subjects: by the mighty (like the Saxon Earl Godwin) and the lowly, and by Dane and Saxon alike. He converted to Christianity and, thereafter, brought the zeal with which he sought Empire into suppressing heathen practices, finishing them forever in this country.

The death of his two sons without issue followed closely on his own untimely death in 1036, and his dream of dynastic Empire crumbled and died with them. In 1042, on the death of his second son, Canute II, the Witan, unchallenged, returned the Crown to the House of Alfred for the last time.

King Canute proving to his courtiers, who believed him omnipotent, that he could not command the sea.

CANUTE, Commanding the Sea to Retire.

Preparing for the Normans

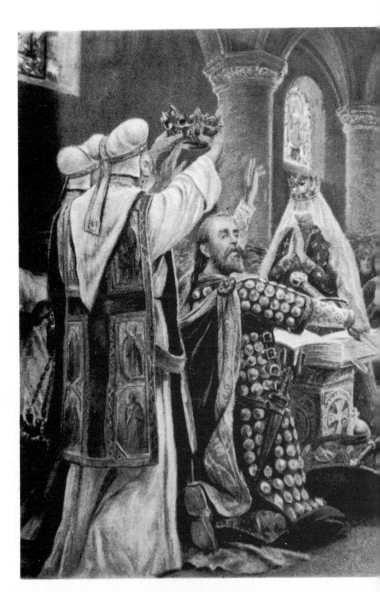

he last descendant of Alfred the Great to be elected King of England was Edward, (1042–1066), known as 'The Confessor', and, sadly, a true son of Ethelred, differing from his father only in his celibacy and his piety. The kindest verdict on him is that he was too pious to be a good king.

Edward surrounded himself with advisers from his beloved Normandy, where he had spent his formative years, to the fury of his most powerful subject, Earl Godwin of Wessex, who succeeded in ejecting most of them from court and country in 1052. Edward forgave neither Godwin nor his son Harold for the part they played in the Norman egress, and, though he was forced, by weight of arms, to accept Harold as his chief adviser on the death of Godwin in 1053, he stubbornly obstructed Harold's policies, playing off the northern earls against him and the other southern earls, but knowing only how to divide, not how to rule. The great work of national unification initiated by Canute was a major casualty of the Confessor's negative kingship, and the fleet wasted and rotted through neglect.

Edward might have been pleased to learn how his life of political and sexual inactivity combined to make the Norman conquest possible, but less happy that it equally completed the decline and fall of the Royal House of Alfred. Edgar the Atheling, although a minor, had the strongest claim to the throne on the Confessor's death in January, 1066, though the Witan instead chose Earl Harold and his proven qualities of leadership, and he, forgetting all oaths of loyalty, accepted in almost indecent haste. His claim to the Crown was tenuous and it paved the way for the equally slender claims of William of Normandy and Harald Hardrada of Norway.

Above Right
The Coronation of Edward the Confessor, 1043.

Right
King Harold (1066), (from a thirteenth century manuscript).

*Edward the Confessor
(1042–1066), (from the
Bayeux Tapestry).*

*Harold and Duke William
together in Normandy, 1064
(from the Bayeux Tapestry).*

The Norman Conquest and the Norman Kings

illiam the Conqueror must have believed
that it was his divinely inspired destiny to
be King of England, for the events leading
to his victory at Hastings and his coronation at
Westminster Abbey on Christmas Day, 1066, are a
maze of conjecture and confusion, conspiring
towards his ambition. How, in 1035, at the age of
seven, did this bastard son of Robert of Normandy
succeed to that dukedom at a period of European
history when illegitimacy was an uncompromising
bar to inheritance? How did he persuade Edward
the Confessor to designate him successor to the
English Crown in 1051? How did he contrive to
extract an oath of allegiance from Harold of Wessex
in 1064, when Harold had his own ambitious
thoughts on the throne of the ailing king? If Harold
had not accepted the Crown in January, 1066, but
sworn allegiance to the Atheling, would William
have invaded? He may then have forfeited the
support of the Pope and much of Europe's chivalry.

If Harald, King of Norway, had not landed in the
north, almost as though orchestrated, with a
massive army of Norsemen just three days before
William's delayed landing at Pevensey, then Harold
of England could have met the Normans with a
fresh, disciplined army eager for the fray, instead of
the bone-weary, depleted band who had force-
marched from their hard-fought victory at
Stamford Bridge. If Harold had, even then, waited
for his levy from Wessex and the tardy, some say
reluctant, reinforcements led by the Earls of
Northumbria and Mercia, the outcome of the battle
may yet have been different. In addition it was very
rare for a king to be killed in battle in the eleventh
and twelfth centuries and Harold's death deprived
the English of the royal presence they needed to
continue unified resistance. London declared for
Edgar, but, as the Norman forces approached in
disciplined triumph, despatched messengers hastily
to welcome the Conqueror and invite him to be
crowned in Westminster Abbey. There was no
further resistance as the powerful northern earls
who had moved so slowly to Harold's aid now
withdrew to their earldoms at a much quicker pace
to await events, erroneously confident that they
were secure in their virtual autonomy.

King Harold's body is brought before the Conqueror, 1066.

William's success was, in small part, due to luck, but it was mostly due to his immense and implacable determination, coupled with moral courage and enhanced by a shrewd military brain, for had he heeded his cautionary counsellors the invasion would never have occurred.

The southern lands of the Godwin family and all who had stood for Harold at Hastings passed in reward to William's Norman followers, among them his uncle, Odo of Bayeux, a great warrior and bishop who spent the latter years of his life in hopeless yet indefatigable pursuit of the Papal Crown.

William paused to build his armed strength and that secured, instructed Edwin and Morcar, the Mercian and Northumbrian earls, that he had determined upon a united kingdom and that they would be part of it whether by mutual agreement or conquest. They rose, as William had intended, and, by inviting the Welsh and Danish to join with them, gave him the perfect excuse to crush them permanently. His army devastated the north and midlands and massacred thousands, both Dane and Saxon. The Norman cruelty and barbarism were long remembered with bitterness, but were equally long effective.

The Danish and French constantly threatened and harassed England and Normandy respectively, and the Conqueror worked with inexhaustible patience and thoroughness to secure unity in the kingdom. His efforts were triumphantly rewarded in the penultimate year of his reign when he took homage and an oath of fealty at Salisbury from 'all the land-holding men who were of any account'. He died in 1087 taking retaliatory action against the French for their harrying raids in Normandy.

William bequeathed Normandy to his eldest son, Robert, and the English crown to his second son, William Rufus (1087–1100). The third son, Henry, was left landless, bitter and jealous and, when brother William was felled by an arrow while hunting in the New Forest in the year 1100, the speed and certainty with which he took the steps necessary to secure his own succession suggested prior knowledge and preparation. He had to move swiftly for brother Robert had a stronger claim to the throne, but the Duke of Normandy was away from Europe on the First Crusade. King Henry (1100–1135) met his brother six years later in battle on Norman soil, defeated him, acquired his duchy, and incarcerated him for the remainder of his long life.

Like his father and brother William before him, Henry ruthlessly maintained unity under his authoritarian rule by swift and cruel suppression at the first sign of baronial unrest or independence. The premature death of Henry's only legitimate son, William, who drowned in the wreck of the White Ship in 1120, caused the deeply grieving king, who himself had usurped the throne, and whose

Coins showing the profiles of Stephen and Matilda.

Robert of Normandy at the First Crusade (c. 1100).

*Death of Harold at the Battle
of Hastings, 1066.*

own father had been a bastard, to lay the seeds for the war of succession that split the country for the nineteen years following his death. He sought baronial support for his obsession that Matilda, his remaining legitimate child, should succeed him in an England where manliness and monarchy were practically synonymous, and ignored his twenty or more lusty and ambitious illegitimate sons, and his legitimate nephew, Stephen, who seemed to epitomize the kingly qualities.

Ironically Stephen (1135–1154) who, with baronial support, usurped the throne in 1135 on Henry's death, had a fatal flaw. Although charismatic, personally courageous and handsome, he suffered habitual indecisiveness; in sharp contrast Matilda, who fought him over the next twenty years, proved her mettle with stubborn courage and in the wisdom she passed to her son, Henry. This period of Civil War was most remarkable for the manner in which both factions abjectly surrendered their power and authority to the barons in return for their irresolute support, so undoing all the unifying work of the three strong Norman kings.

The wars ended when a weary country agreed to accept Matilda's son, Henry Plantagenet, as king on the death of Stephen, in 1154.

Above
*Portrait of Henry I
(1100–1135).*

Right
*Portrait of King Stephen
(1135–1154).*

Death of William II (Rufus),
in the New Forest, 1100.

*The Battle of the Standard in
which Stephen defeated
Matilda, 1138.*

Odo of Bayeux celebrating victory after the Battle of Hastings, 1066, (from the Bayeux Tapestry).

The Early Plantagenets

Henry II (1154–1187), the first Plantagenet ruler of England, was, like many of his descendants, a magnificent specimen of kingship: with his majestic head topped with fiery red hair and his tall, muscular body, he towered physically, as well as mentally, over his contemporaries, and was in every way monarch of the realm. His list of titles, acquired through his mother, his father, Geoffrey, and his wife, Eleanor, was nearly as awesome as his personality, for he was King of England, Duke of Normandy and of Acquitaine, and Count of Anjou.

In the first years of his reign he moved about his new kingdom in impressive armed strength, demolishing the private castles, which had been erected by powerful barons during Stephen's weak and permissive reign, and crushing any signs of incipient rebellion. He then started to shape the administrative system which would, in his life-time, bring unity, order and prosperity to the realm, and to amass wealth for the Crown so considerably enhancing the dynastic prospects of the Plantagenet family. In 1171 he invaded and conquered Eire and added the title Lord of Ireland to his imposing role of names.

In 1173 and 1174 his eldest son, Henry, rebelled, encouraged by his remarkable mother Eleanor of Acquitaine, and aided by the King of France and William the Lion, King of Scotland. But even this array of combined might was insufficient against the strength of the master of England who, having crushed the revolt, invaded Scotland and subjected that kingdom to his power. Further rebellion in 1187 by his son Richard, made Henry's last years bitter and lonely, especially when he learnt, on his death-bed in 1189, of the part played in the revolt by his youngest, and favourite, son, John. The intrigue and rebellions of his sons, which plagued the second half of his reign, were the result of Henry's reluctance to clarify the succession, which created unnatural bitterness between father and sons, and between brother and brother.

Richard (1189–1199) was a great warrior and an heroic figure in his father's image, but he was English by neither up-bringing nor inclination and had an obsessive belief in Christian chivalry; this

Charles le bel recevant la Reine d'Angleterre.

combination of characteristics kept him almost permanently at the Crusades, using his kingdom as his personal treasure chest. The country remained loyal to its absentee king, despite his excessive financial demands, because strong, loyal and able officers, like Hubert Walter, proved and tested the administrative system developed by Henry II and showed it to be solid. Richard visited England for two months in 1194 for the only time after his Coronation, but so great was his fearsome reputation as an avenging Christian, that the leader of a group of rebels, on hearing that the King had landed on England's shores, is said to have died of fright.

Richard died in 1199 fighting alien causes in foreign fields, having named his brother John as successor despite the stronger claim of Arthur of Brittany, the son of their late brother, Geoffrey. John (1199–1216), was handed the Crown despite his unkingly qualities and petty treacheries. He rarely moved events and life just happened to this indolent king. He had been expelled by the Irish in 1185, but it was his puerile antics rather than weighty matters of historical moment that caused the up-rising. In 1204, the strong and gifted French King Phillip II took Normandy and Anjou from a John later capable of no more than vague and ineffective efforts to recover his lost inheritance. William the Lion of Scotland was thereby encouraged to rise against the English yoke and was rewarded by a favourable treaty signed in 1209.

The English barons now took their chance and forced their weak, unmartial king to place his seal to the 'Great Charter' in 1215, and the independence so firmly and painstakingly wrested from them by his great father was returned to them in this one moment of abject humiliation. This final shame forced even the indolent John to action and, with Papal blessing, he repudiated the Charter; at once the 'patriotic' barons invited Louis, Dauphin of France to take the English throne with their blessing and their arms to back him. John died in 1216 with Louis already eagerly on English soil.

Henry III (1216–1272) was only nine years old on the death of his father, John and he ascended the throne to face a daunting mass of armed strength arrayed against him – Alexander of Scotland, the Welsh Llewellyn and the preponderance of the English barons were joined to Louis' cause; the Plantagenet dynasty tottered on the brink of oblivion. But with uncharacteristic foresight before his death John had attracted two influential and decisive forces to his son's cause: firstly, he had obtained Papal support and secondly, he had secured an oath of allegiance to his son from the mighty and chivalrous warrior, William the Marshal. The combination of Pope and Marshal proved sufficient and led to the defeat and humiliation of Louis at the battle of St Bartholomew's Day, 1217. Then, thanks to the

Richard clashes with Saladin during the Crusades (c. 1192).

statesmanlike qualities of the Marshal and the intervention of Stephen Langton, a modified Charter was agreed by both Crown and nobles and uneasy peace returned.

Henry grew to manhood as a true Plantagenet in physical appearance and, though religious and unwarlike, inherited many of the mental qualities of his family. He constantly needed money for building churches, financing Papal projects and fighting incessant wars against the fierce Welsh, and he demanded fiscal support from his barons, blithely disregarding the terms of the Charter and eroding baronial independence. These constant demands ultimately drove the barons to rebellion under Simon de Montfort in 1258, and after six years of semi-civil war, de Montfort won a great victory over Henry's son Edward at the battle of Lewes and Henry became his prisoner. In 1265 Simon summoned a parliament, which has been called the first modern parliament though peopled entirely by privileged and powerful landowners and churchmen; but later in the same year, Prince Edward gained brilliant revenge for Lewes at the battle of Evesham where de Montfort met his death.

Edward (1272–1307) took over the reins of government in 1267 with his father's consent, and by the time Henry died in 1272 was in firm control of the country. He was the first king of England to inherit by virtue of his status as the first-born son of the former king, but proved in his own right to be one of the great English monarchs. He possessed enormous energy, a brilliant tactical ability and a driving ambition to forge a united Britain.

Edward's dream of British unity was a dream of federation, with native Scottish and Welsh kings paying homage to him as their overlord and presenting a united island front to invading forces from across the water.

His Welsh campaigns between 1277 and 1284 were landmarked by his own military genius, the death of the fearless Welsh leader, Llewellyn ap

Right
Portrait of Henry II, first Plantagenet King of England (1154–1187).

Below Left
John Balliol, King of Scotland (1292–1297).

Below Right
The Coronation of Edward I, 1274.

*The Barons forcing King
John to sign the Magna
Carta, 1215.*

Griffith in 1282, and the final conquest of North
Wales in 1284 culminating in the execution of the
last Cymric Prince of Wales, David. Edward had an
unremitting and terrible view of justice and believed
that the Welsh prince deserved to die as a traitor for
being untrue to his oath of allegiance.

Edward's plans for Scotland started well, with the
betrothal of his son, Edward of Caernarvon, Prince
of Wales, to Margaret, the Maid of Norway who was
the acknowledged heir to the Scottish throne. But
she died in 1290 leaving her country without a
monarch. King Edward was asked to choose the
next king for Scotland and, in 1292, made the
unwise choice of John Balliol who, too weak to
oppose Edward, was unacceptable to the magnates,
and, too weak to oppose his magnates, was
unacceptable to Edward.

Meanwhile Philip IV of France, frustrated in his
own plans to invade England by the strength of
Edward's army and navy, intrigued with the
dicontented Scots; at the same time in England, the
barons were becoming restless under Edward,
resenting the money he required for his
interminable wars and demanding their rights
under the famous Charter. The stage was thus set
for a series of Scottish confrontations during
Edward's final years and well into the reign of his far
less able son, Edward II (1307–1327).

Edward I conquered Scotland in a brilliant five
month campaign early in 1297, but later in the same
year, taking advantage of his absence in Flanders,
the Scots rebelled under William Wallace and,
thanks to the bickering and incompetent leadership
of the English barons, defeated Earl Warenne at the
battle of Stirling Bridge. Edward returned in 1299
and salvaged English pride by out-generalling
Wallace at the battle of Falkirk. It was not until 1304,
however, that Edward reconquered the troublesome
country to the north of his borders.

He died in 1307 still campaigning, and from the
moment of his death his son was proclaimed King
Edward II, expressing for the first time the theme of
continuous monarchy. The new king resembled his
father physically, but was the most unwarlike of
monarchs and temperamentally incapable of coping
with the Scottish and baronial problems he had
inherited. His peace-loving nature and the disunity
caused by his quarrelsome magnates, led to a
resurgence of Scottish resistance under Robert the
Bruce and Edward's personal humiliation as a
general at the overwhelming Scots victory of
Bannockburn in 1314. Finally, after an interval of
virtual regency by his incompetent cousin, Thomas
of Lancaster, and a further unhappy period of his
own rule, he was deposed by his estranged and bitter
wife Isabella and her lover, Roger Mortimer who, in
1327, placed Edward's own son on the throne as
Edward III, and, later in the same year, arranged the
brutal murder of the ex-king.

*Monument to Llewellyn ap
Griffith, Prince of Wales,
killed in 1282.*

Left

Effigy of Henry III (1207–1272) in Westminster Abbey.

Right

Effigy of King John (1199–1216), from his tomb in Worcester Cathedral.

Effigy of the ill-fated Edward II (1307–1327) from his tomb in Gloucester Cathedral.

Richard I (Coeur de Lion) executing prisoners during the Crusades (1189–1192).

The Battle of Bannockburn, 1314.

The Hundred Years' War and The War of the Roses

Edward (1327–1377) was only fourteen when he was acclaimed king, yet, within four years, he began to show the characteristics which were to mark his strong kingship. In 1330 he was decisive and courageous, cunning and guileful when he organized the coup which sent his mother's paramour, Mortimer, to summary execution for causing dissension between Edward II and his wife, whilst Isabella herself was forced into unwelcome retirement.

Scottish fighting plagued the early years of Edward's reign, and, once, when he found himself facing an invading Scottish army across a river, he showed his great chivalry by offering to retire some way so that his opponents could fight on equal footing! Then, in 1333, he satisfactorily avenged his father's humiliation at Bannockburn and won a fine tactical victory over the enemy at Halidon Hill.

It was France, however, that dominated his life, for, through his mother, he had a valid claim to the French throne which had been filed formally, though none-too-seriously, in 1328. When, however, the French king Philip VI interfered in Anglo-Scottish affairs and then, in 1336, threatened to invade England with his large French fleet prowling and menacing the English Channel, parliament voted Edward massive sums for the defence of England. The invasion never materialised, but Edward used the money to seize the initiative and, declaring himself the rightful King of France, invaded and began the titanic and tragic struggle which has become known to history as the 'Hundred Years' War'

The period to 1360 is highlighted by two famous English victories. In 1346 at the Battle of Crecy, a mighty French army under King Philip confronted a smaller English force under Edward, but the English king proved the superior general and gained a resounding and prestigious victory, and in the following year successfully laid siege to the key stronghold of Calais. Ten years after Crecy, the English and French armies again faced each other, but under different royal leaders, at the Battle of Poitiers. The French were led by King John, and the English by Edward's first-born son, Edward, Prince

Effigy of Edward, Prince of Wales, ('The Black Prince'), in Canterbury Cathedral.

Edward III crossing the Somme in the face of the French Army, before the Battle of Crecy, 1346.

of Wales and first Duke of Cornwall, known as the Black Prince. This latest Plantagenet proved as chivalrous and able a war-leader as his father and, triumphantly sweeping the enemy army aside, completed the French humiliation by capturing their King, and taking him hostage. In 1360 the French were forced to seek and obtain a treaty by which they ceded large territories to England and there followed nine years of uneasy peace.

By the time a querulous Edward yet again declared himself King of France in 1369, the political stage had altered and England's glory was behind her for at least two generations to come. Not only was King Edward prematurely ageing at fifty-six, but his son, the famed Black Prince was slowly dying and he returned to England in 1370 to live out his last six years quietly with his family. The fighting continued intermittently into the minority of Richard II which followed the death of Edward in 1377.

The expense of the wars continued but, with no royal leaders of military ability, there were no victories, only set-backs and defeats. The only royal personage of stature was John of Gaunt, the oldest surviving son of Edward, but, though an able administrator, he lacked military experience and was unable, therefore, to gain the confidence of the country. In this climate, when the government tried to extort a further shilling per head, the people rose in rebellion in Essex and Kent. Electing Wat Tyler as their leader, they marched on London and were there confounded by the dignity and courage of their young Plantagenet king, Richard (1377–1399) who, at fourteen, met them with a small band of unarmed councillors and persuaded them to disperse, even after their leader, Tyler, was accidentally killed.

Richard, son of the Black Prince, showed the finest qualities of his family in the fantastic drama of the Peasants' Revolt and looked set to be a new Edward I or Henry II but, after peace was signed with France in 1381, he was destined to take up arms thrice only, once against the Scots and twice against the Irish and to fight only in the first Irish campaign. He was a just and good king and a highly civilized man who believed in an almost divine royal prerogative, but, without the respect which could only come from leadership proven on the field of battle, he was unable to command the unswerving loyalty of either magnates or family for his autocratic rule. Eventually, in 1399, whilst he was away on his second Irish expedition, his exiled cousin, Henry Bolinbroke, son of John of Gaunt, landed with an army and deposed Richard as his own army deserted him. He was probably put to death on Henry's orders in the following year.

Henry IV (1399–1413) lived out his reign tormented by the guilt of his regicide and constantly pursued by his cousin's ghost, as the legitimists

The Battle of Poitiers, 1356.

strove against him to place Richard's legitimate successor, the young Edmund Mortimer, Earl of March, on the throne. Even major rebellions inspired by self-interest were clothed in the respectability of legitimism: Owen Glendower, who proclaimed himself Prince of Wales and was a constant thorn in Henry's flesh, worked closely with the Mortimer family, and the greedy Percys whose armed support had helped Henry acquire the throne, now unsatisfied with their rewards, rebelled in favour of the Earl of March. Henry proved far better than his enemies in generalship and, moving swiftly and decisively, crushed the main Percy army under Harry Hotspur and his uncle, Thomas, at Shrewsbury in 1405 before Hotspur's father, the Earl of Northumberland, could come to their aid.

Henry's final, gloomy, years of life were spent bedridden and racked with pain while rebellion remained a constant, rumbling threat just below the surface. Henry V (1413–1422) ascending the throne at the vital age of twenty-six, instantly dispelled the clouds of doom and divine retribution that had pervaded his father's court. He made peace overtures to the legitimists by bringing Richard II's body from Langley to Westminster for ceremonial burial and bribing them with lands, and was, to a great extent, successful. He had shown his martial abilities early when he had contained the ambitions of his rival for the title Prince of Wales, Owen Glendower, and he now began to show himself to be a great Plantagenet in the early heroic and chivalrous mould.

He set about unifying the country by focusing attention on the traditional enemy, France, and succeeded, by a series of subtle political intrigues, to manoeuvre himself into a position where he could invade with some pretence to self-righteous anger. In 1415, on St. Crispin's Day, Henry met the French army at Agincourt with a numerically much inferior force, and the rashness of the French nobility combined with his military genius made it a triumphant and famous victory for England. After a further five years of continuous victories on French soil, the Treaty of Troyes was signed in 1420 whereby Henry would marry Catherine, daughter of the French king, and the throne of France would go to Henry and his heirs forever, on the death of her father, Charles VI. Henry consolidated his great triumphs by continuing the subjugation of French towns during the last two years of his reign.

On Henry's untimely death in 1422, his one-year-old son became Henry VI of England (1422–1461 & 1470–71) and two months later, on the death of Charles, became King of France. John, Duke of Bedford, Henry V's most able brother, became regent in France and continued his brother's policies of subjugation for the next twelve years, initially with great success, but the tide turned with the arrival of Joan of Arc in 1428 and became a torrent running away from the English on the death

The Battle of Crecy, 1346.

Above Right
Effigy of Henry IV (1399–1413) in Canterbury Cathedral.

Right
John of Gaunt being entertained by John I of Portugal (c. 1386).

of Bedford in 1435. By 1450 all but Calais had been lost. The King had grown to majority a kindly, ascetic incompetent, relying on others' advice; there were no royal war-leaders of stature to unify the country. Once again a combination of military failure and weak kingship produced unrest.

'The Wars of the Roses' can be dated from Jack Cade's Revolt in 1450 in favour of Richard, Duke of York, the legitimate successor to Richard II and, over the next eleven years, the fortunes of war fluctuated between the Royal Houses of Lancaster and York. Henry's wife, Margaret of Anjou was the most formidable Lancastrian, whilst Richard Neville, Earl of Warwick was an important force on the Yorkist side. It was, however, Edward, son of the late Duke of York, who, at eighteen showed shrewd generalship when he decisively overcame Margaret's troops at the Battle of Towton in 1461, and, as she fled the field with Henry, took the throne as King Edward IV.

Edward (1461–1470 & 1471–1483) spent the first nine years of his reign attempting to keep his squabbling barons in order. Then, in 1470, Warwick, 'The Kingmaker', pointlessly restored Henry to the throne, but it was the last time he interfered for, in the following April, Edward returned to England and outgeneralled and killed him at the Battle of Barnet. Three weeks later Edward met Margaret at the Battle of Tewkesbury, and, with the help of his warrior brother, Richard, Duke of Gloucester, gained his final, brilliant victory over her. Margaret was imprisoned and Henry died mysteriously in the Tower shortly thereafter.

Edward then looked to France, for he had now realised that England was at its most secure and united when the King was fighting overseas, but the face of European politics was changing quickly and the wily Louis XI of France put off the invading Edward with a favourable treaty, so buying the time to strengthen his own position. By 1479 Louis felt strong enough to send a force to his Scottish ally, thus keeping Edward and Gloucester occupied in the north of the island while he completed his conquest of Burgundy, which he had achieved by 1482. From now on England faced a formidable, united France across the Channel.

When Edward died in April 1483 his son was proclaimed king as Edward V, but Richard of Gloucester had military control of London and had been (reluctantly?) convinced that his brother's children were illegitimate. He, therefore placed his nephews in the Tower and took the Crown as Richard III (1483–1485). His reign was almost as short as that of his poor nephew, for his exiled Lancastrian cousin, Henry Tudor claimed the throne and, landing at Milford Haven in August 1485, met Richard at the Battle of Bosworth.

RICARDVS · III · ANG · REX ·

Portrait of Richard III (1483–1485).

Capture of Queen Margaret after the Battle of Tewkesbury, 1471.

Henry VI at the Battle of
Barnet, 1471.

Although Richard was probably the better general, the issue was decided when the uncommitted Lord Stanley put his army at Henry's disposal and Richard died on the battlefield, the last English king to die fighting.

Richard III and Henry Tudor clash during the Battle of Bosworth, 1485.

Below
*Portrait of Richard Neville,
Earl of Warwick, ('The
Kingmaker').*

Right
*Edward V and his brother,
Richard of York ('The
Princes in the Tower').*

The brave young Richard II riding through London to quell Wat Tyler's rebellion, 1381.

Henry VI, during the Battle of Towton, 1461.

Henry V, reviewing his troops before the Battle of Agincourt, 1415.

*Death of Harry 'Hotspur' at
the Battle of Shrewsbury,
1403.*

The Battle of Towton, 1461.

The
Tudors and
the
Island Kingdom

Henry VII (1485–1509) usurped the throne of an England exhausted by one hundred and twenty years of almost continuous warfare which had left the monarchy humbled and the people bewildered and leaderless. Over the previous twenty-five years four kings had been deposed and only one, Edward IV, had died peacefully. Henry proved just the man to restore stability to Crown and country, for, though merely a competent soldier and neither heroic nor chivalrous, he was a ruthless and avaricious calculator who schemed and plotted a finality to Yorkist aspirations. He took Elizabeth of York as his queen, wove the white rose of York with the red rose of Lancaster to form the Tudor rose, and, when all else failed, put his Yorkist rivals to death.

Henry faced his first crisis in 1487. John, Earl of Lincoln, a nephew of Edward IV and Richard III, landed with a Germano-Irish army and with the imposter, Lambert Simnel, whom Lincoln believed to be his cousin, the legitimate Yorkist claimant, Edward, Earl of Warwick. Henry outgeneralled and killed the Earl of Lincoln at the Battle of Stoke. It has been conjectured that Henry, not Richard III, murdered the young Princes in the Tower, but it is certain that in 1499 he had the wretched Warwick executed, and it was the rebellion of a second imposter, Perkin Warbeck, in 1497, which led to the event. Warbeck landed in Cornwall and recruiting on the way, reached Exeter with six thousand men, claiming to be Richard of York, the younger Prince in the Tower, but his nerve gave and he fled before the King's army. When captured he was imprisoned with Warwick and it was their conspiracy to escape in 1499, which sealed the fate of both men.

In foreign matters, the Valois of France and the Hapsburgs of Germany and Spain were dominating Europe and, fortunately for England, expending their energies fighting each other for control of the Continent. Henry made only one armed expedition to Europe, in 1492, and, though he achieved minimal military success, he exploited the power struggle there to gain great financial rewards. Before the Warbeck uprising in 1497, the King had raised an army to invade Scotland, but a Cornish rebellion resulted from the onerous taxes extorted to pay for

the campaign and so, when Henry had used the
army to suppress the Cornishmen at Blackheath, he
disbanded it.

The last years of his life were spent in relative
peace whilst he amassed a personal fortune, but he
did give the country its first permanent professional
fighting force, the Yeomen, although they were to
be only two hundred and fifty strong in time of
peace. By the time of his death in 1509 he had
transformed England into a prosperous and stable
island kingdom.

Henry VIII (1509–1547) was only eighteen when he
succeeded his father. He was a handsome,
renaissance prince who, for the first twenty years of
his reign, spent his time in foreign wars, pageantry
and sport, whilst his chief minister, Cardinal Wolsey,
ably administered the country. The wars, though
economically unsound, gave Henry great personal
popularity, in particular when he led an English
army to victory at the Battle of the Spur in 1513,
celebrated at the time as another Agincourt. Further
rejoicing came just three weeks later when, at
Flodden Field, another army under the aged Earl of
Surrey, inflicted a crushing defeat on the Scots.

The popularity that Henry courted and gained in
the years to 1530 was to prove essential to him and
the throne throughout the deeply troubled times of
the second half of his reign. The problems of the
succession, which became Henry's overwhelming
obsession, coincided with an insular xenophobia
which became widespread among the English
during the sixteenth century. Henry's need to deny
papal authority in the question of his marriage to
Catherine of Aragon perfectly suited this rising tide
of feeling, especially when the Pope became the
temporal prisoner of the Emperor Charles V. In
1536 the north rose in a serious rebellion, known as
the Pilgrimage of Grace, against the dissolution of
the monasteries, and it was only with the solid
support of the rest of the country that Henry
retained his throne.

The Catholic countries of Europe postured and
threatened invasion, but could not stop their own
squabbles for long enough to turn those threats into
action, and, meanwhile, Henry concentrated the
resources of the nation into building a strong Royal
Navy to defend England against all invaders. It was a
great personal achievement and when, in 1547,
France finally tore herself away from continental
strife for long enough to attack, England's navy
proved itself superior.

Henry's last years were spent in personal decay as
the body politic also rotted. In 1538 he had, at last,
been granted the male heir he had so single-
mindedly sought, and spent his declining years
showering gifts on the family of Jane Seymour who
had lost her life giving birth to his son. Meanwhile
minor rebellions continuously erupted through the
length and breadth of the country as his popularity,
like his life, ebbed away.

Silver groat showing profile of Henry VII (1485–1509).

The Bataile of Spvrs. anno. 1513.

*The Scots hearing the news of
the English victory at
Flodden, 1513.*

The Battle of the Spur, 1513.

When Edward VI (1547–1553) came to the throne, aged nine, Thomas Seymour, Duke of Somerset, assumed power and was named Protector. The series of revolts that had plagued the last years of Henry's reign now cohered in one large uprising called Ket's Rebellion, in 1549. The uprising was not aimed against the young King, and Somerset, who had some sympathy with its cause, treated the rebels with kindness and understanding, but the opposition, led by John Dudley, Duke of Northumberland, sought stronger remedies and, impeaching Protector Somerset, took over the government and quelled the rebellion ruthlessly.

Edward VI showed signs of becoming the most formidable of all the Tudor monarchs before it became clear that he would not outlive his minority. Northumberland, on realising the imminence of Edward's death, forced him to sign a document excluding Henry VIII's two daughters from the succession and making Lady Jane Grey his heir – she was a remote member of the royal family who also happened to be Northumberland's daughter-in-law. The people of London did not countenance the 'will' for one moment and Northumberland and the pathetic young Lady Jane just had time to acknowledge Mary Tudor (1553–1558) as their new Queen before they lost their heads.

Mary I's accession was greeted with great rejoicing and good-will by her people despite her sex (she was the first woman to rule a united England in her own right) and her Catholic convictions. She was determined, however, to have an heir and rushed into an unpopular marriage with King Philip of Spain, anathema to the English as a foreigner and a Catholic, this rash contract proving as barren and wretched as the remainder of her short reign.

When Thomas Stafford revived a long-forgotten claim to the Crown and was recognised by the King of France as the rightful English king, Mary felt reluctantly obliged to declare war in June, 1557. It was a highly unpopular war and money to pay for it had to be forcibly extracted from the people. Mary's final disgrace came on 8th January, 1558, when Calais fell to the French and England lost her last foot-hold on continental Europe. She is reputed to have said on her deathbed, "When I am dead and opened, you shall find 'Calais' lying in my heart".

Elizabeth I (1558–1603) found her country's patience exhausted by the arrogant, autocratic rule practised by her father in his later years and continued by Northumberland and Mary Tudor. Elizabeth determined to be less wilful, to serve her people both as a majestic symbol of their unity and as a pragmatic ruler, for she was aware, almost instinctively, of the growth of parliamentary power and influence in the realm. She strove ceaselessly to be the monarch of and for the people, and she succeeded superbly, save in one area, for she remained obdurately unmarried and provided no Tudor heir for her kingdom.

Far Left
*Portrait of Elizabeth I
(1558–1603).*

Left
*Portrait of Mary, Queen of
Scots.*

Below Left
*Portrait of Jane Seymour by
Holbein.*

Below
*Portrait of Edward VI
(1547–1553).*

Below Right
*Portrait of Mary I
(1553–1558).*

Her accession coincided with England's traditional enemy, Scotland, seeking new alliances and, in 1559, a new page was written in Anglo-Scottish history when an English army crossed the border to help its Scottish ally to oust the unwelcome French. Elizabeth's only Scottish problem was her legitimate successor, Mary Stuart, (Queen of Scots), who, rejected by her own country for her wanton excesses, sought to overthrow her English cousin, only to become her prisoner for nineteen years, until one foolish conspiracy too many, in 1587, forced the reluctant English Queen to order her cousin's execution.

Elizabeth found that the Royal fleet had been allowed to disintegrate between the death of Henry and her accession and she ordered it to be urgently rebuilt, foreseeing the threat of Spanish aggression. By the beginning of the Spanish war in 1585, England's ships were once again seaworthy and Sir Francis Drake could pursue his purpose to 'singe the King of Spain's beard'.

All was but a prelude to the awesome and terrifying sight of the invading Spanish Armada off the English coast as it made its majestic progress up the Channel on the 19th July, 1558. But the great Queen was equal to the imminent crisis and, at Tilbury, made this stirring speech to her troops who apprehensively awaited the arrival of the Armada:

> "... I am come among you ... to live and die amongst you all ... I know that I have the body of a weak and feeble woman, but I have the heart and stomach of a king, and a King of England too ... I will myself take up arms. I myself will be your general, judge and rewarder of every one of your virtues in the field".

Sir Francis Drake hearing of the Spanish Armada whilst playing bowls at Plymouth.

The sacrifice of her own life proved, of course, unnecessary, for, whilst the prospects seemed to overwhelmingly favour Spain, England and Elizabeth humiliated the proud Spanish nation by a great and famous victory.

The glorious defeat of the Armada was the crowning triumph for Elizabeth and her people, and the fifteen years to follow were an anticlimax of unrest whilst the fickle nation began to anticipate the accession of her Scottish successor. Her last words, however, addressed to her people remain as a remarkable contrast to those of her sister.

> "I have reigned with your loves ... It is not my desire to live and reign longer than my life and reign shall be for your good. And though you have had, and may have, many mightier and wiser princes ... yet you have never had, nor shall have any that will love you better."

The French capture Calais,
1558.

Elizabeth I addressing her
troops at Tilbury with the
Armada in sight, 1588.

The Armada facing the English Fleet, 1588.

Sold by J. Pine, in King Street near St Anne's Church Soho.

The Divine Right of Kings and Parliaments

James I (1603–1625), son of Mary, Queen of Scots, and already James VI of Scotland, ascended the English throne as the first Stuart king, to much rejoicing and good-will, which soon turned to sullen mistrust as he tried to stamp his authoritarian view of kingship upon a parliament fluttering its fledgling wings of independence. Parliament sought for itself sole authority to levy taxes, thereby controlling military and foreign policy, and it was only James' deep dislike of all matters military that deferred the struggle between king and parliament until the reign of his son, Charles. The Royal Navy was disgracefully neglected by both James and his parliaments and was allowed to decay and disintegrate while the Dutch took the opportunity to gain control of the seas and build their powerful maritime empire.

In 1624, the peace-loving James was reluctantly forced to declare war on Spain when his son's suit for the Spanish Infanta's hand was rejected in an abrupt and humiliating manner, and for once Parliament supported the King, although it sought to restrict the scope and dictate the method of warfare by voting a small levy and attaching conditions to the use of the money. James, and his adviser and favourite, George Villiers, Duke of Buckingham, had chosen to ignore these attempted restraints and to pursue their own more expansive and expensive war, when James died leaving Charles and his inherited favourite to face the inquisition of Parliament.

Charles I (1625–1649) started his reign badly by telling his Parliament that the poor peace resulting from the desultory and disastrous war was not its business and promptly dissolving it when it sought to argue. The King's military 'policy', before and after Buckingham's assassination in 1628, was both unco-ordinated and unsuccessful, driving parliament into great antipathy so that it made extreme demands on the King before voting him money. Moderate men, such as Sir Thomas Wentworth, later to become Earl of Stafford, concerned at the growing hysteria of parliament, moved to the King's side. In 1629 the King felt strong enough to dismiss Parliament, and he ruled without one for eleven years.

Portrait of Charles I (1625–1649).

*Portrait of James I
(1603–1625).*

Charles equitably levied 'ship money' on his own authority to rebuild the Royal Navy, and, by 1635, it was once more a power to be reckoned with. Sadly, however, the King's military and foreign policy continued to bé bitty, unpopular and, most unforgivable of all, unsuccessful. In 1638 he backed Archbishop Laud's plan to force the Anglican Prayer Book on the Scots and faced the awesome might and terrible anger of the Scottish National Covenant. After early defeat, Charles hurriedly called the Earl of Stafford from his tyrannical governance of the Irish, to form and lead the army against the Scots, and Stafford agreed provided that a parliament was called to approve the levy. When the first Parliament for eleven years was called it refused the money, but, when it was discovered that some of the members were in touch with the enemy, the King received Stafford's backing to dissolve the 'Short Parliament'.

On the 28th of August, 1640, the English army under Stafford was routed by the advancing Scots at Newburn, and Charles was compelled to call a parliament, destined to be his last, to authorise the compensation demanded by the victorious army. Parliament successfully sought the impeachment and execution of Stafford and, in October 1641, John Pym raised the question of Charles' own fitness to rule. After a short struggle for power in London, highlighted by the King's vacillations, he fled his capital in January 1642, to return only for his trial in 1648. The first Civil War had begun.

In the initial stages of the War it seemed that the daring and inventive cavalry leadership of the King's nephew, the glamorous Prince Rupert might prove decisive – for Parliament had no outstanding generals, but the Navy, so strengthened by the King and his ship money, turned on its saviour and joined the Parliamentarians. The battle of Edgehill in September 1642, though giving victory to neither side, forced the Royalists to withdraw to Oxford which remained their headquarters until the end of the war. The next major battle was fought at Marston Moor on July 2nd, 1644, when the vastly superior numbers of the Parliament forces, coupled with the discipline of Oliver Cromwell's 'Ironsides', combined to defeat the courageous Rupert. The King's cause was not yet lost, however, and a Royalist Army in Scotland, under the Marquis of Montrose, won some remarkable victories before the 'New Model Army' under Sir Thomas Fairfax and Cromwell conclusively defeated the forces of the King at the battle of Naseby on the 14th June, 1645.

The remaining three and a half years of Charles' life were spent as a prisoner whilst he played political games which seemed channelled towards one end, – his own martyrdom. If this was his intention he succeeded when he gave his life with great dignity on the 30th January, 1649.

Oliver Cromwell at the Battle of Marston Moor, 1644.

Earl of Stafford on the way to his execution, 1641.

*Scottish Covenanters crossing
the border into England,
c. 1638.*

E.B.L.

Execution of Charles I at Whitehall, 30th January, 1649.

Prince Rupert charging at the
Battle of Edgehill, 1642.

Charles I on the eve of the
Battle of Naseby, 1645.

The Stuart Restoration

The Dutch Fleet at the mouth of the Thames, 1667.

The Royalist cause remained popular in Ireland and Scotland until Cromwell had cruelly crushed the Irish at Drogheda and Wexford in 1649, and turned his attention to Scotland, where, in 1650, the Covananters had invited Charles, son of the executed King, to become their monarch. Cromwell met the Scottish forces, led by David Leslie, at the battle of Dunbar on 3rd September 1650, gaining an indecisive victory, then, one year later to the day, surrounded and overwhelmed an invading Scottish army, with Charles at the head of his own troop, at the battle of Worcester. The young King fled and, after the Oak Tree incident, made his way to France to await events.

Charles II (1660–1685) was invited to return by General Monk at the head of his army, to an England which had never been reconciled to the illegality of Cromwell's Protectorate, and he was warmly welcomed as a constitutional monarch who had accepted, under the Declaration of Breda, that unparliamentary taxes were unlawful. He found that Cromwell's unwitting legacy to him included a large, efficient army which, though mostly disbanded in 1661, formed the nucleus for the English standing army, and a powerful navy.

A commercial war was fought against the Dutch in 1665 and although James, Duke of York, Charles' younger brother, and Prince Rupert had some initial naval successes, James' inexperience and inability as a naval commander led to humiliation in 1667 when the Dutch fleet under Admiral de Ruyter took the English flagship the *Royal Charles* in tow to Holland and terrified Londoners by cruising the mouth of the Thames, whilst the English fleet was in dock.

The nation recognized the changing constitutional position of the monarch when the Earl of Clarendon, as chief minister, was made the scapegoat for the Dutch debacle, and Charles thankfully sacrificed his old adviser, but it was the King's own admiration for Louis XIV, the 'Sun King' of France that led to the start of his second Dutch war in 1672. Under their young and determined leader, William of Orange, the Dutch defended dourly against the might of France and

Edw.d Spragge
e Dutch Fleet from
h of the Thames.
ly 23 · 1667.

England, and, when the combined Anglo-French fleet was held by the genius of de Ruyter at Southwold Bay, Parliament forced a Charles, desperate for money, to approve the Test Act of 1673 preventing Catholics from holding office. This Act smoked out the King's own brother and successor, the Duke of York, who was forced to resign as Lord High Admiral.

The final years of Charles' reign saw the start of party politics in parliament as the Court (Tory) party upheld the King's insistence that his brother James should succeed, whilst the Country (Whig) party under the leadership of the Earl of Shaftesbury supported the claim of the Protestant, but bastard, son of Charles II, James, Duke of Monmouth. Victory came to the Tories because of Whig excesses in their anti-papist propaganda, and when the King died in 1685 he left England with a successor, a standing army and a strong Royal Navy, although his foreign policy had helped to make France the most powerful nation in Europe.

James II (1685–1688) came to the throne with the opposition in confusion, and so when the ill-fated Duke of Monmouth landed in the West Country to claim the throne in May, 1685, James' army under the leadership of the young John Churchill was easily able to defeat him at the battle of Sedgemoor in June 1685.

James began to force his religious views on his unwilling people, who feared an intolerant Catholic dynasty when the Queen gave birth to a son in June 1688. A letter was sent to James' eldest protestant daughter, Mary, and her husband William of Orange, asking them to come to England, and on 5th November 1688 William landed at Torbay and began to march slowly through southern England, provoking none and encouraging no-one to join him, thus forcing James to be the aggressor. James, joining his troops at Salisbury, found them demoralised as their leaders, including Churchill, defected to William and received the final blow when he heard that his second daughter, Anne, had also deserted him. He fled abroad leaving the throne vacant.

William III (1689–1702) and Mary II (1689–1694) ruled jointly through a period dominated by the war with France. French naval strength initially enabled French troops to land in Ireland in 1690 under the leadership of James II, but William met James at the battle of the Boyne in 1st July, 1690 and won a famous and decisive victory. William was himself in the thick of the fighting, while James preferred to observe from a remote hill-top and fled before the battle was over.

The war, which lasted until 1697, re-established English naval superiority at victories such as La Hogue in 1692, but confirmed the invincibility of the French army at battles like Steenkerke in the same year; the latter engagement made the King unpopular when 6000 Englishmen gave their lives

Above
Portrait of Edward Hyde, 1st Earl of Clarendon.

Above Right
Charles II fleeing from the Parliamentarians after the Battle of Worcester, 1651.

Right
Portrait of Mary II (1689–1694).

Far Right
Portrait of Charles II (1660–1685).

under the command of a Dutch general. In 1694 the
Bank of England was founded to finance William's
war, but was made solely responsible to parliament.
It was William's stubborn persistence, coupled with
England's financial strength and naval supremacy,
that forced Louis XIV to sign the Treaty of Ryswick
in 1697, thereby ceding most of France's hard-won
conquests. From then until his death in 1702,
William concentrated on forming a Grand Alliance
against France.

Anne (1702–1714) inherited a great deal from her
brother-in-law: a strong army, which William
himself had shaped, a supreme navy, a healthy
economy and the genius of John Churchill, now Earl
of Marlborough, as her commander-in-chief.
Anne's own contribution to the victories of her
reign, was her infatuation with Churchill's wife,
Sarah, whose influence ensured that her husband
and his political ally, the Earl of Godolphin, were
able initially to have their own way in the ensuing
war.

Marlborough's great victory at Blenheim in 1704
against vastly superior numbers, heralded the end of
French armed dominance in Europe, and with
Admiral Rooke's successful naval engagement at
Malaga in the same year, England was on the
offensive. France reeled under a series of English
and allied victories culminating in 1706 at Ramilles
when Marlborough inflicted a further crushing
defeat. In the meantime at home, the Act of Union
was completed on 1st May 1707 welding those old
enemies, England and Scotland, together.

Continuing defeats forced Louis XIV to sue for
peace in 1707, but Marlborough's harsh terms
caused him to continue the war, and, at the battle of
Malplaquet in 1709, the French, whilst losing the
day, rediscovered their pride. This pyrrhic victory
for England coincided with Sarah's fall from Royal
favour, and the dismissal of her husband in 1711 was
followed by the Peace of Utrecht in 1713, to the
rejoicing and great material benefit of Britain.

*Flight of James II after the
Battle of the Boyne, 1690.*

Left
*The Duke of Monmouth
pleading for his life before
James II after the Battle of
Sedgemoor, 1685.*

*General Monk permitting
excluded members of
Parliament to resume their
seats, just prior to the
Restoration, 1660.*

*William III leading his troops
at the Battle of the Boyne,
1690.*

Profile of Queen Anne
(1702–1714).

*John Churchill, Earl of
Marlborough with his staff at
the Battle of Blenheim, 1704.*

The Battle of La Hogue,
1692.

The Hanoverians

Portrait of George I (1714–1727).

George I (1714–1727) was a great-grandson of James I, but, as Elector of Hanover, spoke no English and was additionally a stupid, unglamorous and brutish man. Many in England would have welcomed the return of James II's son, James, the 'Old Pretender' as James III, if he would but espouse the Protestant faith; even when he refused, the Scots under the Earl of Mar rose in his support in 1715. Mar's army of 8000 men was held by 3500 of Marlborough's veterans at the battle of Sheriffmuir and the rebellion disintegrated when James himself, arriving late, proved to have too little charisma to sustain it. Many Europeans opposed the Hanoverian succession, but after an English naval victory over Spain at the battle of Passaro in 1718, and the death of Hanover's arch-enemy, King Charles XII of Sweden in the same year, the throne was, for the time being safe for George.

With the rise to power of Sir Robert Walpole in 1720, a policy of peace was adopted and sustained with the liberally bribed George I's active support, and when the King died in 1727, Walpole already exerted great influence on his son George II (1727–1760) through the new King's wife, Caroline of Anspach. This period of peace lasted until Walpole's influence began to wane after the death of Caroline in 1737 and opposition pressures for war were vocalised by William Pitt, the Elder. Walpole was forced to declare war against Spain in 1740 but the army and navy were unprepared after twenty years of peace and he was forced to resign in 1742.

George regretted the manner of Walpole's departure and resented Pitt's part in it, and for the next fifteen years, personally obstructed Pitt's great ambitions. George II gained personal glory and a place in history as the last English king to lead troops in battle at Dettingen in 1743, and on the winning side! But the war continued to be waged in a desultory manner and, in 1745, the English troops suffered a severe defeat at the battle of Fontenoy, it was the first set-back for an English army in living memory. In that same year of '45, Charles, grandson of James II and known to history as Bonnie Prince Charlie, landed in Scotland and fired

Sketch of William, Duke of Cumberland (the 'Butcher of Culloden').

Portrait of Prince James Francis Edward Stuart ('The Old Pretender').

Portrait of Sir Robert Walpole.

the Highlanders to fanatical support for the glamorous Stuart dynasty, which he epitomised. They swept south into England as far as Derby before a gathering host of seasoned Redcoats forced them to retreat into Scotland, where, after a victory at Falkirk, they were eventually broken at Culloden on 16 April, 1746, by an English army led by George II's able son, the Duke of Cumberland. The Duke lives in Scottish memory, however, as the man who ordered the indiscriminate slaughter of the Highlanders after his victory.

The war on the continent, whilst no great success for England, ended in the favourable Treaty of Aix-la-Chapelle in 1748, but during the eight years of peace that followed, the indecisive British government allowed the French to 'empire-build'. When war broke out again in 1756 the initial French victories led to the fall of the government and forced the reluctant George to summon Pitt to power. The years from 1757 to the King's death in 1760 saw, for the first time in English history, magnificent and glorious victories inspired by a man who was not King nor had the monarch's support, although George delighted in the victories themselves.

Pitt strengthened the navy and the armies overseas and as early as 1757 tasted the fruits of victory when Robert Clive, aged 32, won India from the French at Plessey with a mixture of cunning and treachery against an enemy numerically twenty times his strength, losing only ten men to gain the sub-continent. In 1759 General James Wolfe, aged 34, stormed the 'heart of the enemy's power', Quebec, and died heroically defeating the equally gallant French general, Montcalm, thus opening the way into French North America, and, in the same year, on the European stage, the English army under Ferdinand of Brunswick, finally avenged Fontenoy at the battle of Minden.

George III (1760–1820) succeeded his grandfather when he was twenty-two and at a time when the power and prestige of Britain had never been greater on the world stage, but he disliked and mistrusted Pitt, and chose his own favourite, the Earl of Bute as his Prime Minister in 1761. In the face of great public outcry the King and his first minister sought peace with France. The Treaty of Paris of 1763, though giving England most of North America, was regarded as a betrayal of Pitt and the expansionists, and set the seal on the obstinate monarch's relations with his people for the next twenty years.

The policy of peace pursued by the King and his succession of ministers between 1763 and 1775 reduced the National Debt, but at the expense of the armed forces, particularly the Royal Navy. By 1770 when the King was using his constitutional powers to the full, and Lord North was forming his ministry of 'The King's Friends', the American colonists were already groaning under the British taxation. But now the obdurate monarch and his obedient

George II leading British troops to victory at the Battle of Dettingen, 1743.

minister insisted on total submission to the English
crown, forcing the Americans to the War of
American Independence, which opened with British
defeat at Lexington in April 1775. Despite victories
like Bunker Hill in June of the same year, the war
moved inexorably America's way. For a time the
French fleet, allied to America, dominated the
English Channel, and the English suffered naval
humiliation when the American John Paul Jones in
Serapis defeated *HMS Countess of Scarborough* in a sea
battle on September 23rd 1779. In 1781 the land war
ended when General Cornwallis capitulated at
Yorktown and the British evacuation began. By the
Treaty of Versailles in 1783 Britain recognized
American independence, but not before she had
salvaged her naval supremacy, some of her pride *and*
the West Indies, when Admiral Rodney defeated the
French at the battle of The Saints on April 12th,
1782.

In twenty years, and almost single-handedly, the
King had brought his country from a pinnacle of
success to the depths of abject failure, and in
December 1783 he turned to the twenty-four year
old William Pitt, (the Younger) to lead the nation out
of its troubles. Pitt's policy of peace over the next
ten years brought stability and prosperity back to
Britain, but left the army and navy in a perilously
low condition.

On January 21st 1793 the French guillotined their
king Louis XVI and, one week later, anticipating
reaction, declared war on Britain to the delight of
George III. The King wished a total commitment to
Bourbon restoration in France and was supported
by Edmund Burke, but Pitt sought only a limited
war to check French aggression and increased
neither taxation nor the armed forces in 1793 so
losing the initiative, whilst Frederick, Duke of York,
George's son, waited in Flanders and in vain for the
support to march on Paris.

The early years of the Napoleonic wars belong to
the Royal Navy. After a serious mutiny had been
quelled in the summer of 1797, the seas were swept
clear of the enemy in a series of brilliant battles:
Viscount Duncan's victory at Camperdown in
October 1797 was so decisive that the Dutch fleet
ceased to exist as an invasion threat; the battle of the
Nile gave Britain mastery of the Mediterranean
when Admiral Horatio Nelson discovered the
French fleet at Aboukir Bay and destroyed it; and
the greatest of them all, the heroic battle at Cape
Trafalgar on October 21st 1805, when Britain faced
Napoleon's Europe entirely alone, Nelson securing a
victory that convinced the world for at least seventy
years thereafter that the British Navy was invincible.

The Duke of York had been made Commander-
In-Chief of the demoralised army in 1795 and it was
thanks to his care and administrative reforms that
the troops did not mutiny with the navy in 1797. He
was also responsible, to a great extent, for the
morale and dicipline of the army that landed at the

*'Redcoats' hunting the routed
Scots after the Battle of
Culloden, 1746.*

The Battle of Minden, 1759.

mouth of the River Tagus in 1808 and continued to fight and win battles like Salamanca (1812) and Vittoria (1813), under the great leadership of Sir Arthur Wellesley (1st Duke of Wellington), until the final showdown between Napoleon and Wellington at the famous battle of Waterloo on June 18th 1815.

In 1815 George III had been hopelessly insane for four years and the country had suffered the unpopular Regency of his son, George, who still had to wait a further five years before succeeding his father as George IV (1820–1830). The new King was to face a reign of domestic turbulence but military peace as he bid fair to be England's most unpopular monarch. His attitude to matters of state may be told in the story of the excited official rushing to tell him of Napoleon's death on St Helena in 1821: "Sire, your greatest enemy is dead!" "Is she, by God!" responded the delighted George, thinking he referred to his estranged wife, Caroline of Brunswick. His popularity is expressed in the Times obituary

> "There never was an individual less regretted by his fellow-creatures than this King. What eye has wept for him? What heart has heaved one sob of unmercenary sorrow?"

William IV (1830–1837) was a simple, bluff and coarse sailor given to plain speaking; and, whilst his reign was peaceful and a time of great social reform, his manner did nothing to repair the damage done to the dignity and majesty of the Crown by his brother George IV. At one New Year's Eve ball, for example, he amazed his guests by taking an old seafaring friend, Admiral Lord Amelius Beauclerk as his dancing partner!

It is not surprising, in the circumstances, that when he died in 1837 respect for the monarchy had never been lower.

Right

Portrait of William Pitt, the Elder, 1st Earl of Chatham.

English forces under General Wolfe storming Quebec, 1759.

*Robert Clive examining the
enemy lines before the Battle
of Plassey, 1759.*

Below
The Battle of Lexington, 1775.

Far Right
Surrender of British General Cornwallis at Yorktown, 1781.

Left
Portrait of Prince Charles Edward Stuart ('Bonnie Prince Charlie' or 'The Young Pretender').

Below
Portrait of George III (1760–1820).

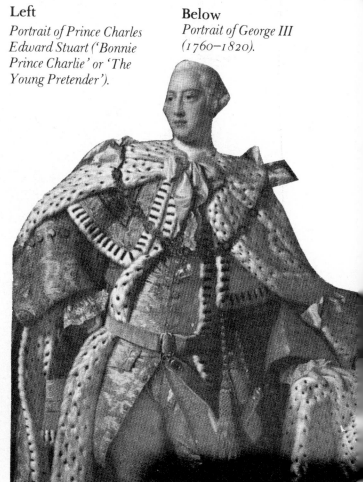

The Battle of Trafalgar,
1805.

*American Admiral John Paul
Jones accepts the surrender of
Captain Pearson of the
Serapis, 1779.*

Napoleon leading a cavalry charge.

Right
Portrait of Frederick, Duke of York.

Below
Etching of George IV described in the caption as: 'A Voluptuary under the horrors of digestion' (1820–1830).

Portrait of Caroline of Brunswick, wife of George IV.

A VOLUPTUARY under the horrors of Digestion.

*Portrait of William IV
(1830–1837).*

The Battle of Waterloo,
1815.

*Nelson receiving the Spanish
Sword after the Battle of
Cape St Vincent, 1797.*

Victoria and Albert

Queen Victoria (1837–1901) succeeded her Uncle William, at the age of eighteen, and faced the formidable task of restoring dignity and majesty to the Royal Family. As the Times said, in describing her welcome by the people of London

> "They thought of her not as an individual … they regarded her as an institution. They saw the monarchy in Queen Victoria and pledged themselves that … they would preserve the monarchy, in spite of an ill-advised monarch."

Victoria's youth, her natural dignity and her fortuitous marriage to Prince Albert of Saxe-Coburg (the Prince Consort) in 1840, gave her the means to repair the damage. She used them fully and to great effect.

In 1845 Baron von Stockmar was still able to advise Albert that "In reference to the Crown, the secret is simply this. Since 1830 the executive power has been entirely in the hands of the Ministry", but during Albert's life the constitutional power of Queen and Consort developed and strengthened because of his undoubted qualities of leadership, unsparing willingness for detailed work and the deserved respect he was afforded by politicians like Lord Palmerston. Albert instilled in Victoria an awareness of her duty to watch over the government and restrain or encourage it, when it proved necessary to do so.

Albert realised that the immediate Royal Family should no longer assume leadership of the armed forces either in the field or administratively, and refused the post of Commander-In-Chief of the Army when it was offered to him, out of genuine respect, by the old Duke of Wellington in 1850. He also, unsuccessfully, opposed the appointment of the Queen's first cousin, George, Duke of Cambridge to that same post in 1856, and was eventually proved right when the choleric conservatism of the Royal Duke deferred long-needed reform in the army until after his enforced resignation in 1895.

The Charge of the Light Brigade during the Battle of Balaclava, 1854.

When the Crimean War, against Russia's imperial ambitions, broke out in 1854, Victoria and her Consort were already playing active roles in the Government. The Roebuck Committee had recommended that the army be made more democratic, but Victoria, believing that the aristocratic elite helped her to retain her own place at the pinnacle of the military pyramid, successfully opposed the proposed reforms. Then, at a Council of War attended by both Victoria and Napoleon III, she was able to persuade the French Emperor not to attempt to lead the Anglo-French troops personally in the Crimea, as the British would never follow a Bonaparte.

The year 1854 saw famous victories for the British and French at Alma in September, and at Balaclava, where the Charge of the Light Brigade and the Charge of the Heavy Brigade are remembered for the stupidity of the generals and the wonderful bravery of the men; it was the very aristocrats whom Victoria supported who caused this military disgrace, yet she defended the memory of the Earl of Raglan, whilst recognizing him for the fool he was. The victory at Inkerman in November ended a year that looked glorious on paper, but stories of the appalling deprivations of the British troops were reaching home. The capitulation of the Russians after the siege of Sebastopol in 1855 virtually ended the war, and the Treaty of Paris followed in 1856.

The Queen was horrified by the stories of conditions in the Crimea and it was one of the reasons she mistakenly appointed her cousin, Cambridge, as Commander-in-Chief of the army, but she did give her total support to Florence Nightingale in her crusade to reform conditions in the military hospitals.

There was glory too to match the horror. The Queen was well aware of the symbolic importance of the medals she gave to her soldiers "I am proud of it", she said, "proud of this tie which links the lowly brave to his sovereign". The proudest moment of all occurred at the great victory parade of 1856, when, dressed in her scarlet military uniform and seated majestically on her horse, Victoria reviewed the march-past of "the largest force of Britishers assembled in England since the battle of Worcester". As one observer recorded at the time "(The) War involved curious ancient bonds between the Army and their monarch."

The new-found powers of the monarchy did not last beyond the death of Prince Albert in 1861, for the Queen found that without his strength she could not prevail against the politicians. She became a virtual recluse for ten to twelve years, and when she returned it was in symbolic majesty as Empress of the glorious British Empire on which the sun never sets. That Empire reached its zenith at the Golden Jubilee in 1887, when the monarchs of the world came to pay homage to her. She had achieved what she set out to achieve; namely to make the Royal

Queen Victoria inspecting the British Fleet in 1849.

Family respected, revered and loved by the British people.

The turn of the century saw her life coming to a close, but before she died she witnessed the outbreak of the Boer War. At first things went badly for the British and after the 'Black Week' series of defeats in 1899, at Stromberg on December 10th, at Magersfontein on December 11th and at Colenso on December 15th, the old Queen may have remembered those 'ancient bonds' from the days of Crimea nearly fifty years before, when she said to Arthur Balfour "We are not interested in the possibilities of defeat – they do not exist."

The great Queen was still actively interested in the progress of the war and had urged the Government to send Lord Kitchener and Lord Roberts to South Africa long before they did. She lived to see the Relief of Ladysmith by Sir Redvers Buller in 1900 and President Kruger, leader of the Boers, fleeing from South Africa in October 1900, before she died in January 1901 knowing that the fortunes of her beloved Britain were once more in the ascendant.

Florence Nightingale with injured soldiers during the Crimean War.

Left
Portrait of Albert, Prince Consort of Queen Victoria.

Right
Early photograph, showing a bastion after it had been stormed by British troops during the siege of Sebastopol, 1855.

*Coronation of Queen
Victoria, 1839.*

Jubilee print celebrating three great British victories of Queen Victoria's reign: Inkerman, Sebastopol and Tel-el-Kebir.

Lords Roberts and Kitchener stepping ashore at Cape Town during the Boer War, January, 1900.

Photograph of President Kruger of Transvaal, leader of the Boers.

*The Battle of Magersfontein,
1899.*

From Saxe-Coburg-Gotha to Windsor

dward VII (1901–1910) spent the greater part of his life subject to the imperious will of his mother, Queen Victoria, and was permitted to perform public functions and study government papers only with her royal consent, which was rarely and begrudgingly given. In consequence he sought refuge from her personal tyranny at the gaming tables and in pursuit of other popular, though more exotic, diversions. The rift between them became self-perpetuating for, as he wallowed deeper in self-pity and self-indulgence, she became ever more convinced of his unworthiness to hold high office. She became concerned for the future of the monarchy, which she had spent her reign restoring to a place of affection, and respect in the hearts and minds of the British people.

At the age of seventeen, Edward was gazetted as an unattached army colonel, and three years later, in 1861, was permitted to join the second battalion of Grenadier Guards in camp at the Curragh. It was soon apparent, however, particularly after the death of his father, Prince Albert, that he would be allowed only nominal command despite his eagerness to serve, his love of the army and his personal courage.

In 1871, the Prince's sudden recovery from a near-fatal illness on the tenth anniversary of his father's death, created a great wave of public sympathy and love for the monarchy, which was used by Victoria and Disraeli to enhance the majesty of the Crown.

On 10th June, 1875, at the age of 33, Edward was made field-marshal, but this placed him no closer to active service and, in 1882, goaded by German cartoons depicting him as a field-marshal whose only experience of fighting was at the annual battle of flowers on the French Riviera, he begged his mother to permit him to take an active part in the Egyptian campaign. Victoria's Personal Secretary, Sir Henry Ponsonby, replied explaining that not only would it be impossible for him to be attached to the expedition on active duty, but unwise for him to even join it as an observer, and that Her Majesty had been so advised by the Government and by 'several leaders of the Opposition'. Edward thereby missed the opportunity to share in the glory won by

Portrait of Edward VII (1901–1910).

Portrait of General George Gordon.

the British army under Sir Garnet Wolseley at the Battle of Tel-el-Kebir in September 1882, when the Egyptian army was annihilated and Egypt left totally exposed to the invading forces of the British Empire.

In 1884, Edward was urging the Government to hasten the mission to Khartoum to relieve the beleaguered General Gordon, and pleading to be allowed to accompany it. His counsel and request were ignored, and the rescue force was despatched tragically late, and without that keenest of all British field-marshals, the Prince of Wales. Gordon died at the hands of the Madhi's forces on 26th January, 1885, just two days before the arrival of the relief mission.

Throughout his life Edward showed the greatest interest in foreign affairs, even though his persistent requests for access to Foreign Office papers were consistently refused by Victoria. As Prince of Wales, he would often take sides in European conflicts. In 1864 he showed overt sympathy for the Danish cause during the Schleswig-Holstein crisis and, in 1870, for the French cause in the Franco-Prussian war, additionally showing much kindness to the newly-exiled Napoleon III after his capitulation at Sedan in September of that year.

He favoured Disraeli's anti-Russian policy between 1876 and 1878, and therefore shared in the Conservative leader's popularity when the Anglo-Turkish agreement signed in June 1878 gave Britain occupation of Cyprus and allowed Disraeli to claim "peace with honour". He was vociferously opposed to Gladstone's policies in South Africa in 1880 and in Egypt and the Sudan in 1884, whilst the first policy may be said to have played some part in Paul Kruger's declaration of the independent Boer Republic of Transvaal in December 1880, the death of General Charles Gordon can certainly be attributed to the latter.

When Edward finally ascended the throne in 1901, after many frustrating years waiting and watching from the wings, he showed remarkable strength of character and determination to bring his own personality to the office of King. He did not seek to achieve the somewhat remote love and respect earned by his mother, tinged as it was with awe, but strove to popularise the monarchy. He revived the pomp and ceremony of royal occasions, having observed the euphoria with which nation and Empire had greeted Victoria's magnificent Jubilee celebrations after years during which she had abandoned these outward symbols of royal majesty.

He immediately created a constitutional crisis by ignoring his more senior ministers and summoning the Secretary of State for War, St. John Brodrick, to a series of audiences aimed at bringing the Boer War to a swift conclusion. It is possible that these meetings brought forward the date of the signing of the Treaty of Vereeniging, by which the Boers acknowledged British sovereignty in 1902, but Edward was forced to bow to Government pressure

Portrait of Admiral of the Fleet, Lord Fisher.

*Edward VII, as Prince of
Wales, firing a Maxim Gun
in 1880.*

and, thereafter, gave formal audience only to his Prime Minister and Foreign Secretary.

Throughout his reign, the King positively and openly supported the army and War Office reforms proposed by Brodrick, and later by Viscount Haldane, in the teeth of strong opposition from entrenched establishment opinion. He showed similar unswerving support for the naval reforms sought so single-mindedly by Admiral of the Fleet, Lord Fisher, and opposed by a similarly determined establishment. Brodrick paid tribute to Edward VII in his memoirs forty years later, praising the excellent results which flowed from his 'uncompromising determination' to see army reform, and adding "the one great monument to King Edward's military interest was the reform of the (army) medical system, which he pressed forward from the first day of his reign".

Edward had always loved travel and this passion accompanied him to the throne. His love affair with France continued unabated and a triumphant visit to Paris in 1903, where he became affectionately known as 'l'oncle de l'Europe', contributed significantly to the signing of the famed Anglo-French 'Entente Cordiale' in April 1904. He often visited his nephews, the weak, vacillating Nicholas II of Russia and the vain, posturing and dangerous Wilhelm II of Germany, seeking to influence them to pursue respectively progressive and non-aggressive policies. Sadly, Edward's undoubted charm and strength of character exerted a democratising influence on the Tsar of Russia only when he was physically present, and successful visits to Portugal, Italy, Austria, Bulgaria and Rumania when added to his French triumph, convinced the jealous paranoic Kaiser that Edward was trying to form a block of hostile nations intended to surround and isolate Germany. There is no evidence to suggest that Edward had any such intention, indeed, it appears that he had but one overwhelming objective; to keep peace in Europe.

The later years of his reign were saddened by his growing awareness that, despite his efforts, a lowering cloud filled with conflict and destruction was darkening the skies of the European continent and creeping menacingly across the Channel threatening to envelop his island Kingdom and then his Empire. Edward had used his limited capabilities untiringly, and his family connections unavailingly, in the cause of peace and he died, an exhausted man, in May 1910, continuing the toil of duty until a few hours before his death.

George V (1910–1936) was, until 1892, content to anticipate a career in his beloved Royal Navy, for it was his elder brother, Prince Albert Victor ('Eddy'), who seemed destined to assume the onerous duties of kingship. George had joined the naval training ship, *Britannia* in 1877 as a twelve-year-old cadet, and then for the three years to 1882 cruised the world

Edward VII, as Prince of Wales, with the officers of the 10th Hussars in India, 1875.

*Edward VII with Tsar
Nicholas II of Russia in
1908.*

with his brother in the training vessel, *HMS Bacchante*. In the next year, aged eighteen, he was separated from Eddy for the first time and, joining the corvette *Canada* for service on the North American Station, was promoted sub-lieutenant on 3rd June, 1884. His naval career progressed through the Royal Naval College, Greenwich, where he secured first-class results, to service on the Mediterranean Station under his uncle and able commander-in-chief, Prince Alfred, Duke of Edinburgh, who profoundly influenced the young prince. George then attained command of the gunboat *Thrush* and, to his great pleasure, was promoted commander in 1891.

His naval career came to an abrupt end on the 14th January, 1892, when his deeply loved brother died, and he was forced to abandon the navy to be bound apprentice to his future career as a constitutional monarch. His progress through the naval ranks, he insisted later, owed nothing to his royal birth, he had earned the promotions on merit and had shown the keenness and aptitude that might have gained him high command.

When Edward VII died in 1910, George and Britain were only four years away from the horror of blundering incompetence and meaningless death, now known as the First World War. His coronation was celebrated on the 22nd June 1911, by the review at Spithead of the largest fleet the world had ever seen. Britain and her new King were flaunting the might of their Empire in an attempt to restrain German imperial ambition.

Before the dangers of war on the Continent became all-absorbing, however, George was deeply disturbed by the threat of a conflict in the west and determined to prevent civil war in Ireland. In 1913 he appealed to all interested parties to practise restraint and, in July 1914, on his own initiative, called a conference at Buckingham Palace which, though failing in its major purpose to reach agreement, created an atmosphere that promised well for future negotiations. Sadly, further meetings had to be indefinitely deferred as those involved turned their eyes to the events unfolding in the east.

George had succeeded in improving relations with the Kaiser for, in 1911, he had invited his grateful German cousin to attend the unveiling of the Queen Victoria monument outside Buckingham Palace and, as late as May 1913, had visited Germany receiving great acclaim as King and Emperor. It was reported that whilst the British and German flags flew proudly from every building in Berlin, the flag of Russia, with the Tsar Nicholas also present, fluttered sadly and solitarily over the Russian Embassy. In 1912 George had warned Prince Henry of Prussia, brother of the Kaiser, that, in the event of Austria and Germany going to war with Russia and France, Britain was committed and determined to assist the latter, and he continued to give these warnings. On July 25th 1914, with war almost

Edward VII in Berlin, 1909.

Edward VII saluting French Regimental Flag at Vincennes in May 1903.

inevitable, he told Prince Henry that England still hoped not to be drawn into conflict and the Kaiser, mistaking the tenor of the King's words, chose to see this as an assurance of neutrality.

On 4th August, 1914, the King, in Privy Council, attended by one minister and two Court officials, sanctioned the proclamation of a State of War with Germany from 11.00 pm. In reality, of course, the decision to declare war had been taken at a Government meeting earlier that same day, when the Cabinet had determined to defend the neutrality of Belgium.

George dedicated himself entirely to the British war effort during the years of confrontation, frequently visiting military units near the front lines and, in 1915, whilst in France meeting troops destined for the trenches, he was thrown from his horse and suffered severe damage to his pelvis. In Britain he toured cities, factories and military establishments indefatigably, and people were encouraged and inspired by his dignified and regal bearing. His passion for the Royal Navy made him particularly proud when his second son, 'Bertie', Prince Albert, serving as a sub-lieutenant on *HMS Collingwood*, was mentioned in despatches after the Battle of Jutland, that naval encounter which, on 1st June 1916, cleared the German fleet from the seas.

The King made personal donations to the exchequer, thereby serving as a model for the country, and also set a moral example by rationing all food and materials used at Buckingham Palace and abstaining from alcohol for the duration of the war. The latter was a sacrifice that Prime Ministers Herbert Asquith and David Lloyd George were unable or unwilling to emulate.

George maintained the closest interest in all appointments to the high command, supporting Kitchener fully until his death in June 1916. He played a secret, but influential, part in the removal of Lord French as commander-in-chief of the British Expeditionary Force in France in 1915, and when Lord Fisher resigned as First Sea Lord in the same year because of the Royal Navy's failure to bombard the Dardanelles into submission, the King passionately believed that the aged Admiral should be hanged as a deserter! George mistakenly sided with Prime Minister Asquith and his inept generals, Robertson and Douglas Haig, against the inspirational Lloyd George, but was finally forced to abandon Asquith and ask the charismatic Welshman to form a government. George then showed himself to be an obstructive and difficult opponent, by promoting Douglas Haig to field marshall to spite his new Prime Minister. He then insisted that Field Marshal Robertson should remain as Chief of Staff, but when Lloyd George offered his resignation, it was the King who capitulated rather than face a constitutional crisis.

The Princes Albert Edward and George (later to become George V) in 1878.

Edward VII with his son,
George V, and his grandson,
Edward VIII, 1909.

George was concerned to lessen the hysterical
anti-German emotion that pervaded the country.
He saw with sorrow and anger the enforced
resignation of Prince Louis of Battenburg as First
Sea Lord less than three months after the outbreak
of the war, simply because this able and royal naval
officer, who had won his rank on merit after forty-
six years of distinguished service with the Royal
Navy, had been born a German and retained his
German name. The King sought, unsuccessfully but
bravely, to save captured German submarine crews
from the disgraceful reprisals visited upon them by a
British people and an Admiralty terrified of these
novel, and German, underwater operations. Even
owners of dachshunds were forced to exercise their
dogs secretly, lest they face the ugly anger of a mob.
The most virulent expression of anti-German
feeling was saved for the royal family itself, however,
when a bitter and irresponsible press campaign in
1917 forced the King to satisfy an angry and
hysterical public by changing the family name from
Saxe-Coburg-Gotha to Windsor at about the same
time as the Battenburgs became Mountbatten.

The change of family name to the Royal House of
Windsor coupled with the obvious devotion to duty
with which King George had laboured for Britain
throughout the war now caught the popular
imagination and, when the Armistice was signed on
11th November, 1918, the royal family and
Buckingham Palace became the natural focal points
for public rejoicing and patriotic emotion.

The clash between the King and Lloyd George
continued and, soon after the Allied victory, the
Prime Minister sought King George's authority to
call an immediate General Election, correctly
believing that his Coalition Party would be
overwhelmingly returned to power by a grateful
nation. The King, convinced that the election should
be deferred until public euphoria at victory and
peace had abated, was forced to give way under
immense pressure and, by allowing the Prime
Minister to choose the date for the election,
relinquished one of the last executive prerogatives
of the Crown. He may have found some consolation
could he have foreseen that the opportunist Lloyd
George would be the last Liberal to hold office as
Prime Minister and that the Liberal Party would be
cast into the political wilderness.

George and Great Britain faced one further
menacing confrontation during his lifetime, when
the General Strike of 1926 threatened to develop
into total civil war with the country irrevocably split
by 'class' and political dogma, until the Trade
Unions finally bowed to the constitutional authority
of the Conservative Government. After the
submission, the King appealed for restraint and 'a
peace that will be lasting', but the Tories, under the
leadership of Stanley Baldwin and Winston
Churchill, were determined to press home their

*Cartoon captioned:
'Brittania Mourns Edward
the Peacemaker', from The
Sphere, May, 1910.*

advantage, and, with the Unions humiliated and bitter, the nation remained widely divided.

When King George was terminally ill in January 1936, the country's respect and affection for her dying monarch was almost tangible, and the future of the British Crown seemed solid and secure. This was almost an irony as, since the war, the monarchic system of government had been collapsing throughout Europe, as Kings and Emperors lost their thrones and their lives. The stability and popularity of the British royal family lay partly in the gradual move towards constitutional monarchy that had taken place over the centuries. Indeed George himself had realised the importance of closing the gap between monarch and people and had been quick to use broadcasting to reach many more than had previously been possible, whilst he and Queen Mary continued those successful royal progressions through Britain which they had initiated during the war. He remained, however, the remote King-Emperor who received the love and respect of his people but was unable, by his nature, to get close to them.

George's eldest son, David, who succeeded him as Edward VIII (1936), had been aware from an early age of the need to be 'in the closest possible touch with the people' and had written to his father in November, 1918 "I'm sure you won't mind when I tell you that I'm out the whole of every day seeing and visiting the troops i.e. the people!!!". This boyish, brave Prince of Wales played a great part in popularising the monarchy and widening its scope beyond the person of the monarch to embrace the entire royal family.

Prince David had joined up at the outbreak of the First World War as an officer of the Grenadier Guards, but was, to his genuine dismay, forbidden both active service and inspection visits to the front line. He protested to Lord Kitchener that he was afraid of neither danger nor death and had four brothers to take his place, to which the great national hero replied that, whilst the Prince of Wales' death would be no important matter, his capture would be a serious embarrassment! The Prince persisted in his attempts to see active service and, though this was not permitted, he was allowed closer to the front line trenches, until the day his driver was killed by a German shell which demolished his car only minutes after he had left it to inspect some troops.

Perhaps more than his personal bravery and considerable boyish charm, it was his obvious deeply-felt compassion for the underprivileged that gave him a special place in the hearts of the British and helped to keep the country at peace during the sociological troubles of the late twenties and early thirties.

The Battle of Jutland, May, 1916.

*George V with his cousin
Kaiser Wilhelm II of
Germany in London in
1911.*

In the final test, however, he lacked the courage to assume the ultimate burden of kingship and abdicated his responsibilities for the love of Mrs Wallis Warfield Simpson. He may also have seen, underlying his younger brother's shyness, the strength of character that would make the Duke of York a far more worthy king.

'Gassed', a painting of British soldiers in the First World War, by J. S. Sargent.

'Dead in Trench', *a painting showing some of the horror of trench warfare in the First World War.*

Left
*Zeppelin shot down over the
English coast, December,
1916.*

Below
*George V with Lord
Kitchener in Port Said.*

*George V with Kitchener
inspecting troops on Salisbury
Plain, November, 1914.*

George V with the King of
the Belgians in Belgium,
1916.

Edward VIII, as Prince of Wales, with his brother, the future George VI, returning from Australia in 1922.

George V and the Prince of Wales visiting the Fleet shortly before it put to sea to receive the surrender of the German Navy, November, 1918.

Edward VIII, as Prince of Wales, in flying kit during his inspection of the Home Fleet,.1932.

*Portrait of Edward VIII
(1936).*

*Edward VIII with his three
brothers, the Dukes of York,
Gloucester and Kent, at his
only Trooping the Colour,
23rd June, 1936.*

Like Father . . .

George VI (1936–1952) was, like his father, the second son of a monarch and a naval officer by training and preference, but in crucial ways he was at a severe disadvantage, as he suffered from chronic ill-health and a deep-rooted shyness outwardly represented by his embarrassing stammer. In addition he had not been trained for kingship.

George had many misgivings about accepting the Crown, one of which was his paternal reluctance to place the strain of successorship upon his young daughter, Elizabeth. He must, therefore, have looked with favour on the suggestion that his youngest brother, the gregarious and healthy Duke of Kent, should ascend the throne as the member of the royal family best fitted to regain popularity for the monarchy after the damaging abdication. He wanted the optimum for country and Crown, however, and, having been convinced that his own accession would best serve the interests of the nation and would demonstrate continuity of succession, he took up the burden with great reluctance, but with an even greater sense of duty.

In 1909, as the fourteen year-old Prince Albert, George had been sent by his father to Osborne, the former home of Queen Victoria which had been given to the Royal Navy by Edward VII, for whom it had gloomy memories. The Prince's academic career at naval college was not distinguished; bottom of his class at Osborne, he only marginally improved on this performance when he later entered Dartmouth. (During the Second World War their mutual lack of academic distinction forged a strong link between King and Prime Minister). Albert joined the Royal Navy as a midshipman in 1913 and, although already plagued by a severe stomach disorder, served as a naval officer until he had seen action aboard *HMS Collingwood* and had been mentioned in dispatches after the Battle of Jutland in 1916. It was decided in 1917 that as the sea exacerbated his gastritis, he should join the Royal Naval Air Service instead, and, after appointment to the newly-formed Royal Air Force in 1918, he qualified as a pilot one year later.

Right
*George VI in airforce uniform
in 1918.*

Left
*George VI, when he was the
Duke of York.*

The Prince was created Duke of York in 1920 and three years later, after a courtship that had its vicissitudes, he was married to Lady Elizabeth Bowes-Lyon. George V sent the young Duke on two important good-will tours which must have seemed like nightmares to this shy man with his disconcerting stammer, but he was aware of the price to be paid for royal birth and privilege and bravely fulfilled his engagements in the Sudan and East Africa in 1924 and in Australia and New Zealand three years later. It must have hurt the sensitive Duke when his natural reserve was compared critically with the ebullience and charisma of his elder brother, the Prince of Wales, who had visited Australasia with great success in 1920. To offset the emotional wounds suffered on the latter visit, his young and beautiful wife had given birth to the Princess Elizabeth Alexandra Mary in 1926, and four years later the Princess Margaret Rose was born.

Soon after the Duke of York had made his agonising decision to accept the Crown, he began to show signs that he was aware of the nation's needs from its constitutional monarchy. Firstly he adopted his father's name, George, thereby showing the continuity of succession, and secondly allowed the date that his brother had chosen for his coronation to stand for his own, indicating that the monarchy was more important than the individual who happened to be King.

George remained full of doubt, however, and privately confessed to Lord Louis Mountbatten "This is terrible, I'm only a naval officer, it's the only thing I know", to which Mountbatten replied "That is a very curious coincidence, for my father (Prince Louis of Battenburg) told me that your father came to him and said almost the same thing and my father answered 'George, you're wrong. There is no more fitting preparation for a King than to have been trained in the Navy'." The new King received an additional boost to his confidence when an Independent Labour Member of Parliament asked the House of Commons to vote for 'some form of republic' to replace the monarchy, and the motion was defeated by the overwhelming majority of 403 votes to 5.

George VI hated everything that the Nazi regime in Germany stood for, unlike the ex-King Edward VIII who, as Duke of Windsor, was received rapturously in Berlin in 1937 and, as late as 1940, continued a dialogue with the Nazis in neutral Portugal. It was decided to get the Duke out of Europe and he was given the office of Governor of the Bahamas for the duration of the war, the last post he was to hold for his country. George did support Neville Chamberlain's policy of appeasement, however, because he remembered too well, along with the majority of his people, the wholesale slaughter of gentle and innocent youth that was the horror of the so-called 'Great' War. By

Right
George VI watching troops of Eastern Command with a Bren anti-aircraft gun in October, 1939.

George VI inspecting the Home Fleet at Weymouth in 1938.

March, 1939, however, he had become convinced
that reasoning diplomacy was being used by Adolf
Hitler to delay, not avoid, confrontation and
supported the stronger line taken by the British
Government against German aggression.

On 3rd September, 1939, he wrote in his diary:
"Today we are at war again, and I am no longer a
midshipman in the Royal Navy." In the evening of
that same day he broadcast, in a voice which after
years of discipline and practice was almost stammer-
free, to the disparate peoples of his world-wide
Empire, rallying them to the royal standard of their
King-Emperor to defend the realm and the
democratic freedoms of people everywhere. He later
wrote in his diary "Hitler went to war with the
knowledge that the whole might of the British
Empire would be against him."

George, like his father before him, backed the
wrong war-horse; he felt that Chamberlain was
badly treated when he was swept from office on a
vote of no confidence in May, 1940, and also would
have preferred to work with Lord Halifax than with
the man chosen by Parliament as the new war
leader. His personal antipathy to Winston Churchill
should be seen in the light of the total support that
the new Premier had given to Edward VIII during
the abdication crisis. In one important respect,
however, George differed from his father, for he did
not long remain blind to the leadership qualities of
his great Prime Minister and, by January, 1941,
could write of Churchill "I could not have a better
Prime Minister." It was a mark of the respect that
each man was developing for the other, a respect
that would later turn into friendship.

During the 'Blitz' on London, when wave after
wave of droning, death-dealing German bombers
unleashed their devastation upon the Capital, there
were many well-meaning advisers who begged the
King and Queen to leave London, or, at least, to
evacuate the Princesses, fearing that the Royal
Family could be killed by the bombs or captured by
the Germans when the invasion came, as it surely
would. Their majesties, however, believed
passionately that their rightful place was by the side
of the London citizens who were suffering the full
effects of this new warfare, which failed to
distinguish between civilian and soldier. They
sought no privileges and, indeed, relinquished the
privilege of evacuation on behalf of their children.
Queen Elizabeth explained their attitude in words
that created an upsurge of public affection: "The
children won't leave without me; I won't leave
without the King; and the King, of course, will never
leave."

It should be remembered that during this period
of the Second World War, the German invasion was
a question of 'when?', not 'whether?', and King
George VI practised revolver shooting in the
grounds of Buckingham Palace, intending to die
there, fighting to the end, when the Nazi invaders

*The Battle of Britain at its
peak, August, 1940.*

George VI talking to Australian soldiers in southern England, July, 1940.

came for him.

After every severe air raid of the Blitz, King George and Queen Elizabeth were out in the streets of their Capital inspecting the destruction and picking their way carefully through the rubble that only the day before had been the treasured homes and precious possessions of bomb-bemused victims who, still stunned, continued to search the debris for the bodies of their relatives and friends. The royal couple tried to raise morale, and, though there was little they could do to comfort those who had lost everything, they did inspire others by their heartfelt compassion and personal courage.

The King and Queen shared with the victims of the Blitz those shattering emotions experienced in times of danger and through loss of property, when, on 13th September, 1940, they were nearly killed in a day-light raid during which two bombs fell on Buckingham Palace. The Queen's reaction showed the royal couple's dedication to their task and their belief in the important part they were playing in the war effort "I am glad we've been bombed", she said, "it makes me feel I can look the East End in the face".

The Royal Family also shared the experience of close family loss when, in 1942, the popular brother of the King, Prince George, Duke of Kent, was killed in an air crash whilst on active service. This man of great personality, charm and zest for living, who had served in the Royal Navy until 1929, successfully sought permission, at the outbreak of the Second World War, to relinquish his honorary title of Air Vice Marshal in order to see active service as a Group Captain in the Royal Air Force. George VI loved him deeply and greatly mourned his death.

The King's broadcasts from the heart of his Empire, delivered in his quiet, deliberate and, by now, stammer-free voice, stirred the British peoples and their allies all over the world and, together with the inspiring speeches of Winston Churchill, gave hope to millions of Europeans oppressed by the huge, black shadow of Hitler's evil Nazi rule of terror.

One role of the King in this great struggle was as old as the monarchy and yet, paradoxically, entirely new. For the first time in warfare the civilian population was in the front-line with the fighting forces and George VI, unarmed and resident in Buckingham Palace, was as much at the centre of the conflict and a rallying point for his people, as Edward III or Henry V had been when they had led their armies to victory at Crecy and Agincourt. It was appropriate that this modern King, heir to a great tradition, should have conceived the idea of a medal to honour the valour of civilians in times of war, designed it himself and named it the George Cross.

The King also had to fulfil the more traditional role of the modern constitutional monarch. Like his father, he interested himself in all aspects of the war

The City of London ablaze around St Paul's Cathedral, 1940.

being waged by the professional soldiers and visited innumerable military units and factories through the length and breadth of Britain. In addition Winston Churchill's sense of history allowed the King to visit every arena of war, provided he was kept well away from the fighting. He visited North Africa in 1943 meeting the troops who had made the victorious advance from El Alamein with Field Marshal Montgomery, and he flew to the island of Malta, which had been awarded the George Cross for its resolute resistance to the seemingly incessant German bombing.

In vain King George pleaded with his Prime Minister to be allowed closer to the centres of conflict, but he had his revenge when the D-Day plans were being discussed, for the stubborn old war leader insisted that he should be with the invading Allied forces when they landed in Normandy on D-Day, 6th June, 1944. The King allowed that it was perfectly alright with him if Churchill joined the troops, but added "If you go, I go too." Neither man was present at the landings, although both visited the troops within days of the Allied invasion of Nazi-held Europe.

George VI and Winston Churchill stood side by side during the Second World War as the twin symbols of British majesty and indomitability, but in addition there was the dignity, humour and sympathetic warmth of Queen Elizabeth which has given her, to this day, a unique place in the hearts of the British people.

On Victory in Europe Day, 8th May, 1945, Buckingham Palace was once again the focal point of patriotic, public celebrations, as it had been in 1918, this time, though, the bulldog figure of Churchill deservedly joined the Royal Family on the balcony. George attended a Service of Thanksgiving at St Paul's Cathedral and received addresses of congratulation from both Houses of Parliament, whilst Winston Churchill declaimed in his inimitable manner that the Royal Family had 'more closely identified themselves with their people in war than had any one of their predecessors'. This view seemed to coincide with the judgment of the nation for the King wrote in his diary "We have been overwhelmed by the kind things people have said over our part in the War. We have only tried to do our duty during these five and a half years".

The King, exhausted by the enormous strain that the war years had placed upon him, sought the tranquillity of family life, but the duties of the monarch barely diminish in times of peace. He went to South Africa early in 1947 on a special good-will tour to thank the peoples of that Dominion for overthrowing their Prime Minister, General Hertzog, in 1939 when he had sought to prevent the country from coming to the aid of Britain in her struggle against the German war-machine. Whilst the tour was exhausting for George, still dogged by

George VI and Queen Elizabeth viewing air raid damage in London, September, 1940.

*The House of Commons
bombed in 1941.*

ill-health, his constant concern was that he was
enjoying the warmth of summer in the southern
hemisphere, whilst his subjects in the British Isles
were suffering severe shortages of fuel and clothing
in a vicious, ice-age winter. He was only dissuaded
from coming back early by Prime Minister Clement
Attlee, pointing out to him that his premature
return would only exaggerate the domestic crisis.

By late 1948 King George was already showing
signs of the deteriorating health from which he
never thereafter recovered, and in the early
morning of 6th February, 1952, he died in his sleep
at Sandringham at the comparatively early age of
fifty-six.

He was a remarkable King, deeply loved by his
people, whom he had served faithfully through a
damaging abdication and the greatest war the world
had ever seen, and, because of his dedication,
determination and courage, the monarchy had
emerged stronger than ever before.

The Duke of Kent joining the
Royal Air Force for active
service as a captain in May,
1940.

British soldiers marching past the King, Queen and Princess Elizabeth outside Buckingham Palace, March, 1944.

*The D-Day Beaches at
Normandy.*

*British troops landing at the
Normandy Beaches, D-Day,
6th June, 1944.*

*George VI and Queen
Elizabeth with the Princesses
Elizabeth and Margaret and
Prime Minister Winston
Churchill, acknowledging the
cheering crowds celebrating
Victory in Europe, 8th May,
1945.*

*George VI and Princess
Elizabeth at the Cenotaph on
Remembrance Day,
November, 1949.*

...Like Daughter

Elizabeth II was just ten years old when she became heir presumptive in 1936 and began to pray every night for the birth of a brother who would automatically take the unwelcome burden from her. She was rigorously trained for her future role as Queen Regnant from this time onward, studying the theory and practice of the British constitutional monarchy while first the shadow and then the substance of the Second World War dominated her formative years.

Elizabeth was thirteen and her sister, Princess Margaret, nine, at the outbreak of the war in 1939, and they spent much of the next six years confined within the grim, cold walls of Windsor Castle and its isolated adult community, because of the real threat of their abduction by invading German paratroopers. The King and Queen watched with sympathy and concern as their teenage daughters experienced all the emotional problems of budding womanhood exacerbated by the absence of contemporaries with whom to share their feelings.

In the earlier years the diversions available to the Princesses were limited. They may have found the air-raids exciting but were not apparently scared, for when they first heard the siren at Windsor they did not rush to the shelter but, on Princess Elizabeth's insistence, stayed in their room until they were properly dressed. One highlight was provided for both girls when, on 13th October, 1940, Elizabeth, with her younger sister beside her, broadcast to the children of the Empire on behalf of all evacuated children (the Princesses had officially been evacuated to 'a house somewhere in the country'). "I can truthfully say to you all", she declared in a high, clear voice betraying no nervousness, "that we children at home are full of cheerfulness and courage ... we are trying to bear our share of the danger and sadness of war. We know, everyone of us, that in the end all will be well". Although these sentiments must have heartened parents and children throughout the world, the young Princess could only speak for herself and her sister, knowing few other children, none of them evacuees.

When Elizabeth reached her eighteenth birthday,
her royal duties increased substantially, and she
carried them out with dedication and dignity – even
when deeply upset by the terrible mental and
physical wounds she witnessed as she sought to
bring some small comfort and cheer into the lives of
limbless, battle-weary men in London's hospitals. In
1945 she finally persuaded her parents to allow her
to share one experience with her contemporaries
when she was permitted to join the Auxiliary
Territorial Service (ATS) as 'Second Subaltern
Elizabeth Alexandra Mary Windsor. Aged eighteen.
Eyes: Blue. Hair: Brown.' She proved herself
competent as both driver and technician, but had
only just completed her basic training when the war
in Europe came to an end.

During the war years, however, the most
memorable occasions for Princess Elizabeth must
have been those days when she received letters
written by Prince Philip of Greece from the various
arenas of war in which he served and, best of all,
when she enjoyed his company at Windsor for
Christmas 1943 and until early 1944 while his ship
was in dock. There was already talk in royal circles of
romance and marriage. Philip was the nephew of
Lord Louis Mountbatten who looked upon him as
the son he never had, and who had introduced him
to the Princess at Dartmouth in 1939, probably
already hoping that this royal meeting might one
day develop into a love match.

Lord Louis' life is the history of royal and military
Britain through the twentieth century. He was born
in 1900 and had been held in the arms of his great
grandmother, Queen Victoria at his christening. At
the age of fourteen he observed the second great
naval review at Spithead in 1914, and, later the same
year, after war had broken out, witnessed the
humiliation of his father, Prince Louis of Battenburg
cast out of office as First Sea Lord by the blind anti-
German hysteria sweeping the country. Lord Louis
now resolved that he would one day become First
Sea Lord himself in order to restore honour and
pride to his family name which had been severely
battered by this shabby treatment, and to avenge his
father whose career had been so cruelly curtailed.

Louis Mountbatten did not see action during the
First World War, although in 1916 he joined
Admiral Beatty's flagship, *Lion*, as a midshipman,
having passed out of Dartmouth earlier that year
eighteenth out of his class of eighty. In 1918 he was
promoted to second-in-command of a patrol-boat
of the type designed to sweep German U-boats from
the sea.

He was already beginning to display those
qualities which would make him one of the greatest
royal war leaders of any age, or any country; self-
discipline, ambition, love and consideration for his
men to which they responded with love and respect,
dedication to the minutest detail, and that
staggering energy which was enough for three or

*Lord Mountbatten exhorting
his men in Colombo, Ceylon,
April, 1945.*

four ordinary men.

In the years between the two world wars his achievements were already sufficient to give him a place in the history books. He was first in his classes in technological and electronic studies at Portsmouth and Dartmouth and followed a full career in the Royal Navy, promoted commander at the youthful age of thirty two and then captain in 1937. He invented an instrument which enabled ships to keep station in convoy and encouraged the inventions of others often in the face of indifference or open hostility from the naval establishment, for example the Gazda gun which defended ships from dive-bomb attacks and was finally introduced to all new ships in 1939 after three years of persistent lobbying by Lord Louis. He learnt to play polo and then wrote the definitive book for beginners.

In 1919, whilst studying at Cambridge, he became a member of the Union, and was chosen to lead the debate against Oxford, a singular honour. He accompanied the Prince of Wales on his triumphant tour of Australia in 1920 and when, as Edward VIII, this friend and cousin abdicated in 1936, the saddened Lord Louis offered his services to the ex-King in exile. He must have been greatly relieved when his unselfish gesture was gently rejected and he could turn to his new king, George VI, offering advice and total loyalty, both of which were gratefully accepted. He married Edwina Ashley in 1922 and during the nineteen twenties became the proud father of two daughters, Patricia and Pamela.

Whilst his relentless pursuit of career and duty throughout the inter-war years would have exhausted most active men, it left him with surplus energy which he used to seek prodigious pleasure, thereby gaining a reputation as an insubstantial play-boy!

By 1941, at the age of 41, Mountbatten had already seen much naval action and had been immortalised in Noel Coward's film 'In Which We Serve'. When his beloved destroyer, *Kelly*, had been mined in the winter of 1939/40, and one terrified stoker had left his station, Lord Louis addressed his crew in words that capture much of the quality of his leadership "Out of 240 men aboard", he said, "239 behaved as they ought to have – as I expected them to do. But one panicked and deserted his post – and his comrades – in the engine room. When he was brought before me, he told me himself that he knew the punishment for deserting his post was death. You'll be surprised to know that I am going to let him off with a caution, and a second one to myself for having failed in four months to impress my personality and my principles on each and all of you ..."

Lord Mountbatten's adventures with the *Kelly* have become legend. When she was torpedoed in May 1940, she settled so deeply in the water that the cruiser *Birmingham* felt obliged to signal

Queen Elizabeth and the Duke of Edinburgh at Trooping the Colour, 11th June, 1953.

Lieutenant Philip Mountbatten, RN, after he became a naturalised British subject in March, 1947.

"ABANDON SHIP I'M GOING TO SINK YOU", to which Lord Louis responded instantly "TRY IT AND I'LL BLOODY WELL SINK YOU!", and he was allowed to bring his limping ship safely to harbour. In May 1941 the *Kelly* was hit for the third and last time when in action in the Mediterranean, and sank taking over half her complement with her. The Captain was rescued unharmed from the sea where he had been busy keeping the morale of his crew high by organising singing. He was greeted in Malta by his relieved nephew, Prince Philip, but his first thoughts were for his men and, before the injured survivors could be treated, he was visiting them in hospital, giving them encouragement, and showing no sign of his own recent exposure to the sea.

Mountbatten's knack of being present at historic scenes, even when not making the history himself, continued when he visited Pearl Harbour in October 1941, just two months before the treacherous Japanese attack. He prophetically remarked upon the astonishing inadequacies of its defences, concluding in amazement "Why even the communication wires of the fighter control system are run above ground!"

He was recalled to Britain by his admirer Winston Churchill to organise co-operation between army, navy and air force as Advisor, Combined Operations and was made commodore. Within six months he had been further promoted to admiral and Chief of Combined Operations with a permanent seat at Chief of Staff meetings. During this period he was responsible for unprecedented co-operation between the services, and enthusiastically initiated or supported all the more original ideas which were to prove themselves in 1944 on and near the beaches of Normandy, including the development of the 'Mulberry' floating harbours which were used to such great effect.

Lord Louis' work as Chief of Combined Operations was recognised most fully in a communication he received from the Normandy beaches just after D-day in June 1944 and signed by six of the greatest Second World War leaders; field Marshals Sir Alan Brooke and Smuts, US Generals Marshall and Arnold, US Admiral King and Winston Churchill himself. It read "Today we visited the British and American armies on the soil of France. We sailed through vast fleets of ships with landing-craft of many types pouring more and more men, vehicles and stores ashore. We saw clearly the manoeuvre in process of rapid development. We have shared our secrets in common and helped each other all we could. We wish to tell you at this moment in your arduous campaign that we realise that much of this remarkable technique, and therefore the success of the venture, has its origin in developments effected by you and your staff of Combined Operations". Mountbatten must have treasured this above all

Earl Mountbatten of Burma taking up his appointment as First Sea Lord and Chief of Naval Staff, 22nd April, 1955.

praise he received for his work during this period of the war.

In 1943 Admiral Lord Mountbatten was made Supreme Commander, South-East Asia, easily the youngest man and the only British naval officer to achieve such distinction during the war. He was supported in this appointment, not only by the British Prime Minister and Chiefs of Staff, but also by President Roosevelt and many of his generals. His brilliant achievements during his nineteen months in South-East Asia concluded his phenomenally successful war and are summed up in Churchill's congratulatory message to him at the end of his campaign in May 1945 "I send you my heartfelt congratulations upon the culminating victory at Rangoon of your Burma campaigns. The hard fighting at Imphal and Kohmina in 1944 prepared the way for the brilliant operations, conducted over a vast range of territory, which have crowned the exertions of the South-East Command in 1945. In honour of these great deeds ... His Majesty the King has commanded that a special decoration, the 'Burma Star' should be struck. ..."

Mountbatten remained in the Far East preparing countries, which had suffered the cruel oppression of Japanese imperial rule, for return to independence or a finite period of western colonialism. His views on Empire coincided with those of the post-war Labour Government in Britain, and he was appointed Viceroy of India in 1947 with instructions to create the climate whereby independence could be granted to the sub-continent by June 1948 at the latest. He achieved this incredible feat in just five months between March and August 1947, thereby minimising the inevitable bloodshed. He had once more made history and had done so whilst he and his wife Edwina had earned the great respect and genuine affection of the peoples of an India which had felt increasingly anti-pathetic to British Imperialism before and during the war. The new Indian Premier, Pandit Nehru, begged him to remain as the first Governor-General and he agreed, albeit with reluctance, for his paramount wish was to return to his naval career as quickly as possible.

When Lord Louis finally left India in June 1948, Clement Attlee felt able to assert with confidence "Appointing Mountbatten was one stroke of mine that was entirely successful; in my opinion no other man could have carried out this tremendous task", and the Labour Prime Minister had no problem in persuading a proud King George VI to create his heroic relative an earl. Lord Louis took the name Earl Mountbatten of Burma.

The newly created Earl sought immediate return to his interrupted naval career and as a modest Vice-Admiral began to serve under his former subordinate, Admiral Sir Arthur Powers, who could not get out of the habit of calling Mountbatten "Sir"! Lord Mountbatten's return to the highest command was swift, sure and merited as he reached

H.M. the Queen and Prince Philip review the RAF during Coronation Year, 1953.

towards that goal he had set himself as a fourteen-year-old cadet. 1949: Fourth Sea Lord. 1952: Commander-in-Chief, Mediterranean Fleet. 1953: Allied Commander-in-Chief, NATO Forces, Mediterranean, (almost certainly no other Briton would have been acceptable to America in this key post). 1955: First Sea Lord.

He had achieved his life-long ambition, but his energy remained undiminished as he sought further challenges. In 1956 he received the highest naval honour when he was promoted Admiral of the Fleet, and in 1959 took on an enormous work-load as Chief of the newly created Defence Staff, set up to co-ordinate and unify the Armed Services; indeed no-one was better qualified for the post.

On 20th November 1947, between presiding over the independence of the Indian sub-continent and resuming his naval career, Lord Mountbatten had proudly attended the marriage of his nephew Philip to Princess Elizabeth. By that time Philip had become a British subject and had been honoured to take his uncle's family name becoming known, simply, as Lieutenant Philip Mountbatten RN. A few days after the wedding, however, King George created him Baron Greenwich, Earl of Merioneth and Duke of Edinburgh.

Prince Philip of Greece had been encouraged by Lord Louis, whom he knew as 'Uncle Dickie', to study for the navy when he had been virtually adopted by Mountbatten in 1938 on the death of Louis' elder brother George, Marquess of Milford Haven. In the spring of 1939, at the age of seventeen, Prince Philip took the examination for Dartmouth and passed sixteenth of the thirty-four who gained entry and by the end of the year had won prizes as best all-round cadet of his term (the King's Dirk), and best cadet in college (the Eardley-Howard-Crockett Prize). He was already showing many of the great qualities of his famous uncle; determination to succeed, self-discipline, charm and enormous energy all combined to stamp him as an indisputable leader of men.

Because he was a national of neutral Greece and a member of the Greek royal family, Prince Philip, now an eighteen-year-old midshipman, was posted in January 1940 far from the arenas of marine confrontation on board the ancient battleship *Ramilles* which was being used to transport Australasian troops to North Africa. When Italy invaded Greece in October 1940, however, Lord Louis was able to use all his undoubted influence to get his nephew transferred to the Mediterranean fleet and, by December, Philip was on board the battleship *Valiant* in charge of a section of search-light patrol – an exposed and dangerous station.

In March 1941, Prince Philip saw action at the Battle of Cape Matapan off the south coast of Crete, when part of the Italian navy, a victim of faulty intelligence from the German High Command, was surprised by the British. Ruthlessly exposed in the

Elizabeth II on her Jubilee walkabout after attending a Thanksgiving Service at St Paul's Cathedral, 7th June, 1977.

Elizabeth II, as Lord High Admiral of the United Kingdom, being piped aboard HMS Bronington when she visited the ship's commander, the Prince of Wales, on his 28th birthday, 14th November, 1976.

harsh glare of the *Valiant*'s searchlights, the Italian cruisers *Zara* and *Fiume* were destroyed. After the action, during which the *Valiant* was holed, Admiral Sir Andrew Cunningham, Commander-in-Chief Mediterranean, mentioned Philip in dispatches, and Rear Admiral Sir Charles Morgan, then captain of the Valiant, reported "Thanks to his (Prince Philip's) alertness and appreciation of the situation we were able to sink in five minutes the two 8-inch gun cruisers". The battle was a decisive victory for the Royal Navy, and the Italian Fleet's next sortie from safe harbour was to surrender.

Prince Philip was aboard the *Valiant* at Alexandria when Lord Louis and the other survivors of the *Kelly* were brought into harbour in May, 1941. At the sight of his uncle's face, smeared with black oil and drawn with grief for his lost crew members, he covered his emotion by greeting him with the comment that he looked like a minstrel, to which Mountbatten, drawing on inhuman reserves of energy, responded by robustly reprimanding Philip for his poor letter-writing record.

Philip was promoted sublieutenant on 1st February 1942 and posted to the destroyer *Wallace*, which was engaged in convoy work and patrolled the North Sea and English Channel in intense, penetrating cold, and ever in danger from the shadowy menace of German U-boat torpedoes. The Prince made an immediately favourable impression on his new captain, and, soon after his twenty-first birthday in June 1942, was promoted to first lieutenant and, by October, was second-in-command of the *Wallace*, a singular achievement and weighty responsibility for one so young.

The Prince's period of active duty ended in late 1943 when the *Wallace* returned to Britain for repairs. The next ten months must have been a time of conflicting emotions for the handsome young naval officer, who, while frustrated in his twin ambitions, to pursue an active part in the world-wide war, and obtain British citizenship (even with the formidable aid of Lord Mountbatten), was able to enjoy the company of the young Princess Elizabeth as their friendship burgeoned into love.

In August 1944 he returned to the Mediterranean as first lieutenant on the new destroyer *Whelp*, which gave support to the Allied forces landing in the South of France. The Whelp was then ordered to join the East Indies Fleet, bringing Philip, for the first time, under the overall command of Lord Louis, then Supreme Commander, South East Asia. Philip spent the remainder of the war in comparative safety, based in an Australia no longer threatened by Japanese Imperial aggression, although he longed to be in a more active arena of the war.

Lord Mountbatten, always in the spotlight of history himself, now ensured that his nephew was by his side on the deck of the *USS Missouri*, to witness the

Elizabeth II's Jubilee firework display in the centre of London, 9th June, 1977.

Princes Charles and Andrew
training for parachute jumps,
1st April, 1978.

formal act of Japanese surrender which took place
on 2nd September, 1945 in Tokyo Bay, just four
weeks after the Americans had dropped the atomic
bomb on Hiroshima. Philip remained with the
Mountbatten staff, assisting his uncle to prepare the
countries of South East Asia for a return to peace,
until January, 1946, when he sailed back to England.

Prince Philip's naval career continued after the
war when he taught petty officers at a new training
school, *HMS Royal Arthur*, Corsham. Following his
marriage in November 1947, he was delighted to be
sent on the Naval Staff Course at Greenwich, for
none could aspire to high office in the Royal Navy
without successfully negotiating this further study
and training course.

Official royal engagements were already
beginning to obtrude into the time Philip could give
to the Royal Navy, especially during the period from
October to December 1948 when King George VI
was indisposed and his own wife was recovering
from the birth of their first child, Prince Charles, on
14th November 1948. The Duke of Edinburgh could
already see the shape of his life to come, but the
King was only fifty-three years of age and he still
hoped to be able to pursue a full naval career for
many years ahead and achieve merited high
command, as husband of the royal heir.

In October 1949, he reported, as first lieutenant
and second-in-command, to the destroyer and
flotilla leader, *Chequers*, which was stationed at Malta
where his wife joined him for Christmas. In July,
1950, just two weeks before the birth of their second
child, Princess Anne, he was promoted Lieutenant
Commander and then, in September, achieved a
great ambition when he was given command of the
frigate, *Magpie*; he began immediately to instil
discipline and purpose into his crew, guiding,
inspiring, driving, controlling and comforting them
as he moulded them into the team that made his
ship *Cock of the Fleet*, enabling him to emulate one of
the early feats of his Uncle Dickie and at an earlier
age than Lord Louis!

In July 1951, the Duke was ordered home to
accompany his wife on a vital tour of Canada, which
his father-in-law was too ill to undertake, and,
although he was unaware of it, this heralded the end
of his active naval career. When he was later forced
to accept the courtesy rank of Air Chief Marshal in
addition to those of Field Marshal and, most
embarrassing of all, Admiral of the Fleet, he
insisted, in the face of government opposition, that
he should at least be able to fly. He won the
argument, and then his wings in the spring of 1953.

When the Princess and her husband were setting
out on their tour of Canada in October 1951, all
Elizabeth's training in self-control was needed as she
said goodbye in public to her greatly loved father.
She had to do so without visible emotion, although
already aware that he was suffering from an

*Prince Charles, as Colonel-in-
Chief of the Parachute
Regiment, at Airborne Forces
Day Parade, 8th July, 1978.*

incurable cancer and there was a strong possibility
they would not see each other again. Both father
and daughter had determined that the Canadians
were not to be disappointed, and when the visit
proved successful, strengthening the
Commonwealth ties of the people of Canada, they
both felt that the potential sacrifice had been
worthwhile.

On the last day of January 1952, Princess Elizabeth
left England, and her father, for another tour; this
time she was to visit East Africa, Australia and New
Zealand, and she must have felt the same sad doubts
as she watched the frail figure of her father, his face
thin and drawn, waving his farewell to her at
London airport. This time her worst fears were to be
realised and one week later she returned to England
as Queen Elizabeth II. She had received the news of
his death, in public, with great composure, but
Philip, inexperienced in royal ways, was visibly
shaken by the news, aware of the awesome burden
he now had to assume as husband of the Queen
Regnant, and realising that his naval aspirations
were at an end.

Even when the young Queen scattered red earth
on her father's coffin, she showed no overt emotion,
though her face was pale with the effort to retain her
public dignity. She finally burst into tears, however,
in the privacy of the car taking her back to Clarence
House after the funeral.

The young Queen Elizabeth's determination to
perform her duties in the highest tradition of the
monarchy became clear during her world tour in
1953/54 when she announced to her subjects in
Australia, in words reminiscent of her great
predecessor, Elizabeth I "It is my resolve that under
God I shall not only rule but serve". One of the first
to fully appreciate her qualities was her old warrior
Prime Minister, Winston Churchill who,
remembering the support he had given Edward VIII
at the time of the abdication crisis, returned from
one of his weekly audiences with her shaking his
head in admiration, "Thank God I was wrong," he
said, "we couldn't possibly have got a better King –
and now this Queen!"

Her Majesty carries on the military traditions of
the Royal Family, well aware of the special
relationship between the armed services and their
monarch, and intent upon forging stronger links
between the two. Her choice to reign as Elizabeth II
was carefully considered, not because it was her
given name, nor just to honour her uniquely
popular mother, but also to remind the country of
the glorious figure of Elizabeth I in all her towering
majesty, addressing her troops at Tilbury under
threat from the Armada. Elizabeth II had, by her
own marriage to the heroic nephew of the great
Lord Mountbatten, brought military glory closer to
the throne. She has carefully retained the symbolism
of the Crown and its military traditions in
ceremonial events like Trooping the Colour, and,

*Following in the footsteps
of his younger brother, Prince
Andrew, the Prince of Wales
receives his parachute wings
at Brize Norton. Prince
Charles has long taken a very
active interest in acquiring
military skills.*

Prince Charles, Colonel-in-Chief of the Parachute Regiment meets two World War II adversaries: Gavin Cadden, with beret, and his German captor, former paratrooper Hans Teske (centre).

practically, was instrumental in creating a new medal for British soldiers who have served with distinction and courage in the tragic troubles of the bitter and embattled lands of Ulster.

The Queen has set herself the virtually impossible task of keeping the Commonwealth intact by remaining a symbol of majesty to diverse countries, each with its own national characteristics, each seeking its own identity after years of British colonialism. These nations have responded to her untiring efforts by gratefully accepting Elizabeth II as Head of the Comonwealth, while rejecting much else that is British. In pursuit of these ends, she is proud of her record as the most-travelled British monarch, though she remains a constant target for the ever-growing host of fanatics, freaks, anarchists and homicidal maniacs which are becoming such a depressingly familiar feature of our modern world.

Shortly before her scheduled visit to Ghana in November, 1961, riots broke out and exploding bombs became an everyday occurrence in that unhappy country, then suffering under the despotic rule of President Kwame Nkrumah. Harold Macmillan's Conservative Government believed that her visit should be cancelled, but the Queen thought otherwise: "If I don't go", she said, "Nkrumah might invite Kruschev and the Government would like that even less". Her Majesty's visit to French Canada in October 1964, bears further witness to her determination and courage when she became the subject of direct assassination threats from extreme French separatists who believed that her presence would seriously endanger their aspirations. Elizabeth refused either to cancel the tour or add to her usual security measures, already aware that she must be physically close to her people in order to retain and increase her popularity in modern democratic society.

In 1979 the success of the Commonwealth Conference in Lusaka was threatened by mounting opposition towards the British Government's supposed attitude to the vexing problem of a Zimbabwe-Rhodesia settlement. The Queen was warned that she was in serious personal danger from fanatics if she attended, but attempts to dissuade her were inevitably doomed to failure, and that great popularity she has patiently acquired over the past twenty-seven years as Head of the Commonwealth, made her presence most effective. Consequently Conservative Prime Minister Margaret Thatcher was able to negotiate in an atmosphere of calm that had seemed impossible to achieve before the conference began.

All members of the immediate Royal Family share the same constant danger as Queen Elizabeth. Princess Anne, for example, will always remember the terrifying day a madman attempted to kidnap her in the Mall. Princess Margaret will remember her 1979 tour of the United States, when a

Earl Mountbatten's last public duty, standing in for Her Majesty the Queen at the final rehearsal for Trooping the Colour, with Prince Charles saluting, on 9th June, 1979.

misquoted comment on Ireland and rumours that
one of Lord Mountbatten's murderers was lurking
furtively in the San Francisco area, put her life in
imminent peril, while she carried out her duties
with the cool dignity we have come to expect from
the entire family. We now take for granted the
courage and determination of the Royal Family in
the face of danger, and the news that Prince Charles
visits troops in Northern Ireland as Colonel-in-Chief
of the Welsh Guards, more a target for the
Provisional IRA than any individual soldier, no
longer merits headlines in our newspapers.

The Prince of Wales has already shown many of
the strong qualities of his father and his great-uncle,
Lord Louis, but he prefers flying to the sea, and
joined the Royal Airforce College in 1971. Even
when he later entered the Royal Navy, he learnt to
fly helicopters at the Royal Navy Air School and
qualified in 1974. He and his younger brother,
Prince Andrew, have also been taught to parachute
jump, but Andrew has since passed his exams for
entry to the Britannia Naval College, Dartmouth at
the age of nineteen and, in the great naval tradition
of his family, is likely to serve in the Royal Navy for
at least twelve years.

Queen Elizabeth's patriotism is, of course, beyond
doubt; for example, in 1956, she was deeply
distressed when the Suez crisis ended in such
pathetic failure for her Britain, once the proud
centre of the greatest empire the world had ever
known, now refusing to face the realities of a post-
war world dominated by the titanic struggle
between the superpowers, Russia and the United
States. The Queen may have had her private doubts
about the wisdom of the venture, but she
desperately wished it to succeed once the decision
was made to embark upon it. It now seems likely
that she was informed that Anthony Blunt was a
traitor in 1964, but, if so, it is certain that she
continued to employ him for one reason only:
because she was persuaded that it was best for the
defence of the realm that the Russians should
remain unaware that the 'fourth man' was not only
uncovered but 'turned'.

When the great Earl Mountbatten of Burma,
'Uncle Dickie', was murdered in so cowardly a
manner in August 1979, every close member of the
Royal Family, united in deep sadness, was present at
the ceremonial funeral in London, hurling defiance
at the Provisional IRA, daring them to strike again.
The faces of all members of the family were pale and
strained as they continued to perform their public
duties with dignity, during this time of extreme
private grief. It was sadly appropriate that Lord
Louis should die at sea, but he would no doubt have
preferred to die at the hand of a less dishonourable
enemy of his Queen and Country. Her Majesty,
daughter of the new style King-patriot who had led
his country so successfully during the Second World
War, and herself the symbol of all that the

*The Royal Guards Colonels,
Prince Charles (Welsh
Guards), Prince Philip
(Grenadiers) and the Duke of
Kent (Scots) at Trooping the
Colour, 16th June, 1979.*

Elizabeth II with Princes Philip and Charles waving to the crowd after Trooping the Colour, 16th June, 1979.

monarchy has come to mean to the British in terms of courage and duty, mourned the last in a tradition of magnificent royal warriors, who had included the Black Prince and Prince Rupert.

Queen Elizabeth has faced a very difficult task in this world of instant news and opinion, where today's statesmen are tomorrow's failures, but she has carefully retained the symbolism of the Crown and its military traditions. At the same time she has transported the monarchy into the last quarter of the twentieth century with her walk-abouts and television appearances, without endangering its inherent Majesty. Her Silver Jubilee in 1977, demonstrated the love and respect in which she is held by the British and by other people who have come into contact with her during her popular world-wide travels.

Elizabeth II in uniform as Colonel-in-Chief of the Scots Guards, followed by the Royal Guards Colonels at Trooping the Colour, 16th June, 1979.

*Admiral Lord
Mountbatten and Vice-
Admiral Fife of the U.S.
Navy overseeing NATO
manoeuvres in the
Mediterranean in 1954.*

*Earl Mountbatten takes a
parade at Sandhurst on
behalf of the Queen, 1955.*

Elizabeth II, Prince Philip, the Queen Mother, Prince Charles, Prince Andrew (wearing the uniform of a Royal Navy midshipman for the first time) and Prince Edward mourn before the flag-draped coffin of Admiral of the Fleet Earl Mountbatten of Burma, 5th September, 1979.

Picture Credits

Our thanks are due to the following who supplied the pictures in this book.

Barnabys Picture Library
Mary Evans Picture Library
Picturepoint
Popperfoto
Press Association Photos
Radio Times Hulton Picture Library
The British Museum
The Mansell Collection
The National Portrait Gallery

Her Majesty the Queen, with Prince Philip, the Queen Mother and other members of the Royal Family standing in front of Westminster Abbey after the funeral service for Lord Mountbatten, 5th September, 1979.